A Rose's Guide:

Golf for women

A Rose's Guide:

Golf for women

MELANIE FALDO

Pelham Books
London

I would like to thank my coach, Nick Meaker, and Steve Baldwin, golf professional and director of golf, and his staff at Redbourn Golf Club, Hertfordshire, for their invaluable assistance in the production of this book.

I would also like to thank Aladdin's Cave of Golf for supplying me with the clothes and equipment featured in this book.

First published in Great Britain in 1986 by
Pelham Books Ltd
27 Wrights Lane
Kensington
London W8

British Library Cataloguing in Publication Data

Faldo, Melanie
Golf for women
1. Golf for women
I. Title
796.352'3 GV966

ISBN 0 7207 1680 2

Designed and produced by Sackville Design Group Ltd
Sackville House, 78 Margaret Street, London W1N 7HB
Art Director: Joyce Chester
Editor: Jennifer Mulherin

Typeset in Plantin by Ace Filmsetting Ltd
Printed and bound in Great Britain by
Hazell Watson and Viney Limited,
Member of the BPCC Group,
Aylesbury, Bucks

Contents

Introduction

Golf is a perplexing and yet tremendously enjoyable sport. For three years of my life I followed my former husband's every shot around most of the great golf courses of the world. I got to know a lot about the game at the professional level, and to experience, at first hand, the pressures that success at the sport can exert, and the consequences. Strangely enough, however, I never tried to play the game – beyond the odd flirtation with 'carpet golf' – until Nick and I separated. I then found that the game was not only perplexing and enjoyable to watch, but also puzzling and good fun to play!

I'm now a self-confessed golf addict – and my all-embracing addiction can be traced to the moment when I first managed to hit a golf ball and get it to fly in the air towards its target, rather than along the ground in an ungainly swerve.

My addiction shows no sign of abating, and it gave birth to this book – which is an attempt to chart the growth of my fascination with the sport, in the hope that other women will take up golf and enjoy it as much as I do.

I once saw the words *No Dogs or Women* emblazoned on the clubhouse door of one of the most renowned and beautiful golf courses in the British Isles. It remains one of the more indelible memories of the time I spent accompanying my former husband around golf courses.

This book is not intended to be an anthem in support of women's lib. Its aim, simply, is to encourage women to take up and enjoy the game of golf. However, in the course of telling my own experiences I hope to dispel a few myths created and perpetuated by male golfers and question a few of the rules created by some of them.

On a practical level, the aim of this book is to teach women the rudiments of golf. I hasten to add that it will not be me who does the teaching but Nick Meaker, the Teaching Professional at the Redbourn Golf Club in Hertfordshire – who painstakingly taught me how to play the game.

The book, then, is as much Nick's as mine, as it is from Nick that all the pearls of wisdom fall. Nick refused to take cover credit, and merely asked that the book be dedicated to club professionals throughout the land. This dedication I am only too happy to make, as without Nick's patient and expert tuition, I would probably still be hacking my way around the short course at Redbourn.

The role of the golf club professional is relatively unsung. Few people have heard of Nick Meaker and his like. Whilst my former husband was enjoying tournament success, Nick was attempting to qualify for the British Open the hard way – by taking valuable time off from his club professional duties to play a series of qualifying tournaments – only to fall at the final qualifying hurdle. Probably Nick Meaker will never be as good a tournament golfer as my former husband. He is, however, a remarkably fine golfer and a brilliant golf teacher – because that is the art he has spent so long learning and become so accomplished at performing. Nick has spent untold hours teaching beginners such as myself to play the game and, most importantly, to gain maximum enjoyment from it. His patient and expert teaching method is the very basis of this book; without him, it could not have been written.

The way I set about learning how to play golf is a way anyone can follow. There are 'Nick Meakers' at almost every golf course in the world. Having received professional instruction, I'm a firm believer that, just as you should have driving lessons before using a car, so you should have lessons from a golf professional before stepping on to a golf course. In fact, the cost of driving and golf lessons is roughly the same but if

The Fall of Man from Heath Robinson's *Humours of Golf*, first published in 1923.

you take group lessons (and Nick, for example, has over 20 women in one of his classes) the cost can be dramatically reduced.

Anyone who has ever swung a club with serious intent will know that the process of 'self analysis' is an integral part of the enjoyment of the game. Golfers always have something to talk about because golf really can be dissected and examined. Essentially, it is a sociable game.

So, if you're a golfing widow who has never stepped on the fairway of a golf course, or a mother desperate to escape the house for a few hours while your children are at school, or a young woman keen to try another, perhaps much more satisfying and enjoyable way to keep fit than those offered by aerobics or weight training, think about playing golf. Golf is great fun; it is not just a game for men, it need not be difficult; and it can be taken up by any woman, whatever her age.

No dogs or women

In 1983, a guide to golf courses was published which detailed that, of the 250 golf courses listed, no less than 104 had restrictions of one sort or another on women. These restrictions ranged from 'Women are not permitted to play' to the less severe but equally annoying, 'Women are not permitted to play on Saturdays, Sundays or Holidays'. It was also noticeable that some clubs permitted their members to take their dogs into the clubhouse but not their wives or non-playing female companions! Why?

The answer is both simple and complex. There is no truly defensible reason why restric-

Heath Robinson illustration of the male golfer, complete with pipe and plus fours. This male stereotype can still be found today.

tions against women should ever have been created in the first place. They were, however, and they reflected the attitudes of an era that is now, thankfully, long gone. That they should still be in existence, and enforced by a few in this day and age is quite simply absurd.

Golf is a game that women can play as effectively as men. Women, in general, may not be able to hit the ball quite as far, but then most golf courses provide Ladies Tees to compensate for this lack of length. In all other aspects of the game, women are the equal of men, and no less a golfer than Gary Player believes women to be better at the short game than men. A former US and British Open winner preferred teaching women because they were more inclined to accept instruction than men. As golf is a game where you have to get the basics right, instruction is essential. Potentially women could be as good, if not better, players than men.

It is a myth that women do not have enough power to play the game well, and 'hold men up on the golf course' by playing badly or slowly. In fact, women tend to be much straighter hitters than men, using the timing and rhythm of their swing to propel the ball rather than the naked aggression which is displayed so proudly by so many men as they try to bludgeon the ball towards the target. Most professionals would agree that a 'good swinger' is always likely to beat a 'hitter', and certainly spend less time in the rough stuff – and money on replacing lost golf balls.

Nick Meaker believes that ladies can teach men much when it comes to swinging a golf club.

Caricature of a lady golfer in the early years of this century. Lady golfers were considered by men to be fearsome creatures.

Left: Typical golf course, showing bunkers, water hazards, rough and fairways.

He feels that because women are not as powerful as men, they consciously realise that to propel the ball they have to rely on tempo, rhythm, balance and timing – unlike men, whose first reaction is, all too often, to try and hit the ball out of sight.

Why women are denied entrance to some golf clubhouses is a mystery known only to a few. In the early nineteenth century when women restricted themselves to playing on putting courses, men had little objection – presumably happy to view such involvement as ladylike enough and of no threat to the exclusively male domain of the golf club. When, however, towards the end of the same century, women decided to play full-length courses, most men, it seems, believed they were intruding on their territory. Rules were thus hurriedly penned and passed to curb the invasion.

It was only after World War II that leading players and writers petitioned for change, and change was only slowly implemented. As late as 1975, the ladies competing in the British Amateur Golf Championship at St Andrews were 'generously' given the courtesy of the clubhouse for the first time. This 'revolutionary action' caused certain male members to resign.

To explain why restrictions are still imposed on women at certain golf clubs, it is helpful to survey briefly the development of the women's game.

Right: Female golfer in 1911. A long skirt, and shirt and tie were often worn by women golfers at that time.

A short history of the women's game

It came as a great surprise to me to learn that women have been associated with the game of golf since the early sixteenth century. The first woman known to be connected with golf was no less a personage than the unfortunate Catherine of Aragon who came to England in 1501 and married Henry VIII in June 1509.

A 'right royal start'

It is documented that Catherine of Aragon was a golf devotee. She experienced a series of ill-fated pregnancies in her attempt to provide Henry with a male heir – having several still-born babies and others that died within a few months. She turned to golf, presumably for solace, saying: "My heart is very good to it", and thus became the first woman golf addict in the history of the game.

Although Catherine introduced certain customs from her native Spain, golf was not one of them. It is thought that the Scots invented the game sometime between 1424 and 1457; by about 1513 it had been adopted by the English – so Catherine was more than likely one of the very first people – let alone women – to play the game of golf. Women were thus off to a 'right royal start'.

Mary, Queen of Scots was also interested in golf. At her trial she was criticised for having played golf two days after the murder of her husband, Darnley, in 1567. It is unlikely that Mary, like Catherine, was seeking solace on the golf course – but rather diverting entertainment, since she is reputed with being fun-loving and frivilous.

History does not record exactly what type of golf the queens were playing nor how good they were at it. It is, however, probable that Mary was, at least indirectly, responsible for the word 'caddie' entering the language. When Mary came to Scotland from France, she brought with her to Edinburgh many of the younger sons of the French aristocracy as pages who were known as *cadets*. At a later date after Mary's death, the word seems to have been used to describe vagrants – people of no fixed address who roamed the streets of the capital in search of work. These *cadets* or 'caddies' (the Scottish pronunciation of the two words being identical) were mostly offered work as messengers carrying and delivering documents, letters and goods of all kinds for a small fee. Thus, when it became necessary to find a name to describe someone who carried golf clubs, caddie seemed an obvious choice.

Golf rapidly increased in popularity – so much so in Scotland that a law was passed in 1608 which threatened anyone who played golf on the Sabbath with imprisonment. Fortunately for the golf-loving Scots, this law was repealed by James VI in 1618.

Interest in golf was not confined to aristocratic women. By 1810 it is known that the fishwives of Musselburgh were showing their skill at golf – and it is claimed that they formed a golfing society as early as 1774. The worthy fishwives, seem, however, to be unusual in their devotion to the game, since the next women enthusiasts appear to have been middle-class ladies of North Berwick who, in the 1830s, met regularly to play a round of golf.

Early golf equipment

The equipment used by the fishwives of Musselburgh was a far cry from what we know today. There were no 'irons' as such, as all golf clubs

Right: Some examples of golf clubs in use at the turn of the century, before they were regularized and numbered as they are today.

were made of wood. Golf balls were made of leather and stuffed with feather, wool, frock, or hair. As you can imagine, they took a very long time to make, and were thus expensive items to lose.

Before World War I, the projectiles hammered round golf courses were made from a variety of materials – no standardisation in the size and weight of the golf ball was truly achieved until the 1920s. In the 1840s, for example, rubber balls appeared but met with few accolades.

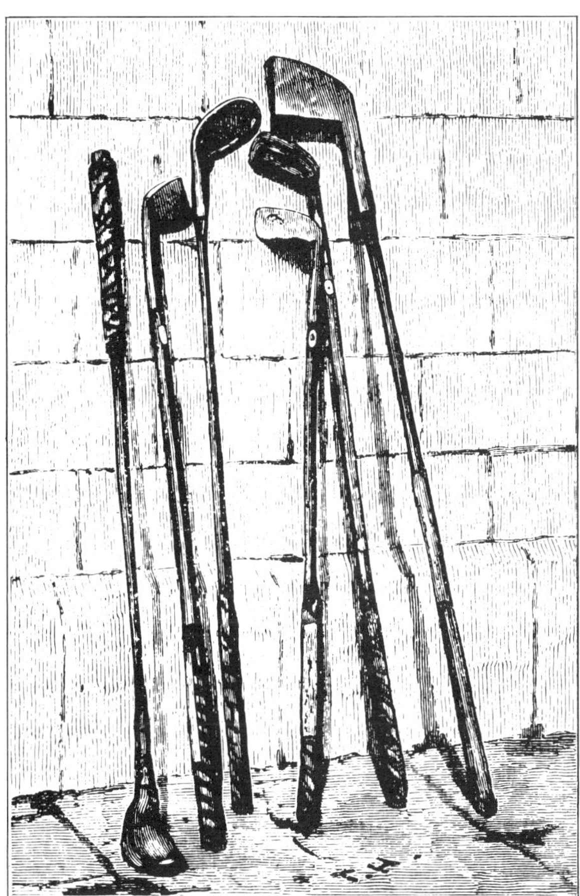

Then, in 1848, gutta percha balls, made from the dried milk of a rubber tree were introduced, but, again, they were unpopular as they did not fly well. Composite gutties were experimented with and met with some success. These, as their name suggests, were made from a variety of materials – most commonly, rubber, cork, and leather.

It was only when the Haskell rubber-core ball was invented in 1902 in the USA that a truly acceptable golf ball was available to the world's clamouring golfers. This ball is justly claimed as the first modern golf ball, and it was made from elastic rubber thread wound tightly round a core. Its drawback was that it was expensive. Despite this, the ball was very favourably received. It met a particularly enthusiastic response from women because, unlike some of its predecessors, it did not demand brute strength to make it fly, but timing.

The development of, first, aluminium-headed golf clubs, and then iron, also helped the women's game to develop. Aluminium golf clubs made their appearance in about 1900 – originally with wooden insets. Steel shafts also made the game easier to play as the shafts were less likely to twist than the hickory that had previously been used. The first patented steel-shafted clubs were legalized in the USA in 1924, and in the UK in 1929.

At the turn of the century, golf clubs were not numbered as they are today, but had an enchanting collection of names. *Mashie Niblick* – roughly equivalent of a 7 iron – is my own personal favourite. The only name that has survived to the present is the *Driver* which, as it is today, was the longest hitting club in the bag. A 2 wood was called a *Brassie* – because it had a brass plate on its bottom to help protect it from stones and earth. The other woods were referred to as *Spoons* – and the 'spoon' of a club was the word

used to refer to the loft of the face of the club. Other names were the *Baffy* – so called because golfers then used to 'baff' the ball towards the hole; the *Mashie* – the rough equivalent of today's 5 iron; the *Jigger* (6 iron); and *Niblick* (9 iron).

Growth of Ladies' Clubs

It would seem that the first 'martyr to the women's golfing cause' is a certain Mrs Wolfe-Murray – who scandalised local folk (especially the men) by playing at the St Andrews links with two clubs in 1855. Women golfers were, at this time and much later, only suffered on the golf course if they limited themselves to putting. 'Two clubs' suggests that Mrs Wolfe-Murray refused to be tied to any such restrictions.

About the time that Mrs Wolfe-Murray was scandalising the people of St Andrews, many women were seeking to end the restrictive nature of their lives. Although the female emancipation movement was in its infancy, one of its by-products was that women began to take up sports which had been almost exclusively played by men. Many women had been golfing spectators – even presenters of trophies and prizes – for years but it was only in the second half of the last century that they took up the game in earnest and in considerable numbers. In 1867 the first Ladies' Club was formed at St Andrews, 250 years after the formation of the men's first golfing society.

The recognition of the St Andrews Ladies' Golf Club was, however, a promising beginning

Ladies putting at the Westward Ho! Ladies Golf Club at Bideford, Devon, in 1873, five years after their club was formed.

– even if the women's game, as documented at the time, was limited to putting strokes only. From this point, the development of the ladies' game can be said to have been steady rather than spectacular.

The ladies of Westward Ho!, North Devon, followed the innovators at St Andrews by forming a Ladies Club in 1868. Predictably, only one club, a putter was permitted. By the end of the next decade, only three more ladies' golf clubs had been formed – to make a grand total of five – but all were limited to the putting courses with the full courses remaining the exclusive territory of men.

The 1880s saw the formation of 14 new clubs and the practice of playing for small prizes. It also saw women refusing to bow quite as obsequiously to the dictates of men by extending their previously limited repertoire. They abandoned the sole use of the putter and began to use the full swing of the golf club.

The women's game in general also finally began to pick up momentum. By the time the Ladies Golf Union (LGU) was formed in Britain in 1893, there were more than 50 ladies' golf clubs. Remarkably, by 1898, this number had increased to 220 – and the women's game was well and truly on the march.

Within a short period, a ladies' circuit was formed with organised championships and international matches.

As a governing body, the LGU grew in strength to become a formidable organisation in women's golf, with the member clubs enthusiastically voting and participating in the legislation.

This was largely due to the zeal of one of the most remarkable women of the period, Issette Pearson Miller, a member of the Wimbledon Ladies' Golf Club and first honorary secretary of the LGU. A tireless organiser in the Union, she encouraged the development of the women's game by helping to introduce the handicap system and setting up many championships and tournaments. Furthermore, the LGU under her aegis, promoted the interests of the game of golf as well as ensuring uniform application of the rules.

Establishment of ELGA

The LGU continued to grow in influence, as did the number of clubs affiliated to it. By 1912 there were over 500 clubs and by 1950 1,249. Dissension, however, occurred in November 1951 when a breakaway group was formed under the presidency of Lady Heathcoat, formerly Joyce Wethered.

Today, this group, the English Ladies' Golf Association (ELGA), has well over 1,000 clubs affiliated to it, and nearly 100,000 members. It manages all its own affairs, except the handicapping system which remains with the LGU.

The LGU itself carried on regardless and, during the 1960s, was recognised as the female equivalent of the R & A. It was not, however, without its detractors. In 1970, for example, a former British Open Champion stated publicly that the women on the Council of the LGU belonged to a different generation from the players and, on occasions, spoke almost a foreign language. The implication was that the LGU was not moving with the times.

The amateur/professional debate

Throughout its history, the LGU has had one overriding problem – the interpretation of what constitutes amateur status. This thorny problem has done much to curtail the development of the women's game in Great Britain. In the United States, professionalism developed at a much earlier stage – with the result that the women's

Enid Wilson, one of Britain's most promising golfers and three times winner of the Ladies' British Open Amateur Championship, seen here at Marylands, Romford in 1938.

game in North America is far more advanced and profitable than in Europe – although the latter is, at last, beginning to create a credible and viable professional circuit.

It seems remarkable that the first Ladies' British Open Amateur Championship was held as long ago as 1893. Yet women had to wait until 1976 for the first Ladies' British Open Championship – open to both professionals and amateurs alike. Even the United States did not host the premiere event in women's golf until 1946 – when the US Women's Open was inaugurated. It was adopted by the US Golf Association in 1953.

Why the women's game has taken so very long to establish itself in Europe is easy to chart but difficult to understand. Just after the turn of the century, women were competing in many county matches, as well as international matches. The most famous of these – the Curtis Cup – developed from a match first staged at Cromer in Norfolk in 1905. The Cup was so called because this inaugural international match between the United States and Britain involved a pair of sisters with the surname, Curtis. It was not, however, until 1932 that the Curtis Cup proper was first played at Wentworth in Surrey. The British team at the time boasted the formidable Joyce Wethered and Enid Wilson, but the Americans won – and this trend has been continued with increasing US dominance overthe ensuing years. The Cup is held every two years on alternating home soil, and Britain had to wait until 1952 for their first victory at Muirfield. Since 1956, the Cup has been held continuously by the Americans. Perhaps the time is ripe for a European team – as is the case in the Ryder Cup!

Professional women golfers have always been excluded from the Curtis Cup, and for many years they, quite simply, did not exist as it was impossible to make a living from the game. Foreign travel in the early part of the century was prohibitively expensive so, international experience was limited to the women who could afford it. When the golfers had to meet their own expenses, talent and expertise took second place in team selection.

All the major tournaments were amateur – and this amateur status was strictly enforced. This placed many leading women golfers in an intolerable position. By attempting to make money in one of the few professional tournaments, they excluded themselves from the more prestigious amateur events. If they retained their amateur status, then the fledgling professional tour would continue to be lack-lustre and generate little media interest. The LGU's interpretation of what constituted 'amateur' status also went beyond the golf course, and this made life extremely difficult for those with talent, yet limited funds.

Enid Wilson, for example, who won the Ladies' British Open Amateur Championship no less than three times, was refused entry to the Royal Porthcawl Championship of 1933 because she had written instructional captions for a series of published photographs. Because she had been paid for the work, the LGU declared that she was no longer eligible to be an amateur. This seemed particularly harsh since she had been writing articles for six years.

Enid Wilson thus left the amateur game at the age of 24, to take up a job at a top sports shop. She went on to spend a lifetime writing about golf, when she might well have been playing it.

The first US Women's Open Championship in 1946 gave the women's game in North America just the exposure it needed. Even today, the Championship runs very successfully without the aid of the sponsors' money – and this reflects

the immense popularity of the women's game in North America. Unfortunately, in Europe, would-be professionals had no such 'flagship tournament' until 30 years after the Americans.

Professional golf for women

An attempt was made in 1953 to launch the first women's professional tournament in Britain, but few women were willing to risk endangering their amateur status when the financial rewards offered were so meagre. At this time, women were, in theory, allowed to act as club professionals. One or two were fortunate enough to find such positions and enjoy the life of a professional, but there were very few tournaments for them to compete in.

Throughout the 1950s, the LGU offered no system of sponsorship nor developed any organised or authorised way for young players to get financial assistance. Finally, in 1962, women were allowed to join the Professional Golfers' Association (PGA), which had been founded a full 60 years before for men. This enabled women to become full members of the PGA after serving an apprenticeship in clubs as professionals or assistants. They were also allowed to register as playing professionals, and compete for the PGA tournament prize money six months after being accepted.

Despite this welcome advance, women golfers in Europe still struggled to make a living because there were very few club jobs for women. There was little sponsorship of tournaments, and the LGU continued to guard its amateur status regulations with strictness. Those few women golfers who took the plunge and turned professional soon found the water much too chilly.

For European women golfers, the American tour offered the only hope of making money. Unfortunately, its standard was so high that even the very best European women such as Vivien Saunders and Michelle Walker struggled against more finely tuned opposition. Vivien Saunders, in particular, disliked the American way of life, and, as there was no comparable European tour, supplemented her earnings by writing.

A short history of the women's game

The Colgate Ladies Professional Golfers' Association Championship played at Sunningdale for the first time in 1975 did prove that a professional circuit would enhance the women's game in Europe. But the LGU-inaugurated Ladies British Open (made possible by a generous anonymous donor, and then through sponsorship by Pretty Polly) did not open a great many doors for Europe's aspiring women golfers. Until Vivien Saunders launched the Women's Professional Golf Association in 1978, none of the 32 major fixtures on the golfing calendar catered for women professionals.

The WPGA was launched when Vivien Saunders persuaded 20 top women players to turn professional and it has, in a relatively short time, proved to be exactly what women's professional golf in Europe needed. In 1985, the Women's European Golf Tour was worth over £568,000, and its leading money winner, Laura Davies, won a not inconsiderable £21,736 in prize money alone. In 1986, the total prize money increased by 25 per cent.

Future of women's professional golf

Now, when compared with the financial rewards of the American women's circuit or the men's European Tour, these figures are still small. The Women's European Tour does, however, offer top women golfers a *living* – and it is gaining momentum with every year that passes. This is vital to the future of the women's game in Europe as, although money isn't everything, it certainly is a great motivator!

The more youngsters who believe they can make it into the women's professional ranks – and be rewarded adequately for their expertise and efforts – then the more girls and young women we will have playing the golf courses of Europe.

Women's professional golf in Europe is on the ascendant. The women's tour over the last couple of years has received more media coverage than at any previous time. It still lacks, however, that large public interest which television coverage alone seems to provide. With television coverage assured – in comes the sponsor's money, increased interest in the women's game, and bigger crowds at the tournaments. More and more women will then be able to achieve a sensible living from the professional tour, and the more women the tour can happily accommodate, then the more women there will be trying to break into the professional ranks. It is perhaps a sad fact, but money talks.

Despite all this talk about professionalism and the growth of the women's game golf is, and I stress again, a game to be enjoyed. I myself will certainly not be joining the ranks of the professionals, unless there is a dramatic and unbelievable improvement in my game – my first target is to achieve a recognised handicap. I have become addicted to the game because it is challenging and great fun to play. Exposure for the women's professional game on television, would, however, provide a welcome boost to the women's game, and make the golf courses that do not exactly open their arms to women members – or offer them the same facilities – think again. The women's professional tour will, in the near future I am convinced, begin to achieve parity with the men's.

Some people would disagree and argue that the public wants and expects to see Severiano Ballesteros thunder the ball away, not an 8-stone woman stroke it delicately down the middle. In my opinion, this is nonsense. There is much more to golf than crunching the ball miles down the middle – although that admittedly is a great sight, and even greater fun if you can do it your-

self. People, I believe, watch golf because it is a game where tempo, rhythm, timing, skill and touch are displayed by professionals – both men and women – in a remarkable way. Once you have played golf, and realise just what is involved, you can but marvel at the way a top woman professional such as Nancy Lopez of the USA can play the game.

Golf is also a very exciting competitive game – whether played by men, women, or in an event in which both play. In the men's game, the public knows and supports its particular favourites. Once the personalites of the women's game become familiar to the public, then the sport will be just as exciting – not withstanding the booming drives of the men (of which more than a few women – Laura Davies is an outstanding example – are more than capable).

I believe that once the television companies start consistently covering the Women's European Tour, and the public gets to know and support some of the already incredibly skilled and extremely colourful personalities in the game, then its popularity as a mass market spectator sport will grow enormously. Finally, women have one great advantage over men – they are often both more graceful players, and more attractive to the eye. This, too, might play a part in increasing the game's popularity.

Left: Nancy Lopez, the outstanding US professional and one of the richest women in the sport today.

Europe's leading ladies

The women described in the following pages finished in the top ten of the European Order of Merit in 1985. The information has been supplied by the Women's Professional Golf Association.

1. Laura Davies

More has been written about Laura Davies than any other player in their first year as a professional. Noted for her power play, she achieved the unique double in 1985 of becoming the Ring and Brymer Order of Merit winner and Rookie of the Year. Her other successes include second place in the Hennessy Cognac Ladies' Cup in May 1985, followed by another second place in the McEwan's Lager Wirral Caldy Classic. Laura's impressive debut on the tour reached its climax when she won the Belgian Ladies' Open, her first tour title.

Sponsor representation: IBM
Turned professional: 1985
Tournaments entered: 19
Top ten finishes: 10
Best performance: winner Belgian Ladies' Open

Year	Order of Merit	Prize money
1985	1	£21,736

Tour victories:
1985 Belgian Ladies' Open

2. Jane Connachan

As an amateur, Jane set the record of being the youngest player ever to compete in the Curtis Cup – she was just 16. In her first year as a professional in 1984, her performances promised to improve on the successes of her amateur career: she finished 8th in the Merit lists. She got off to a fine start to the season in 1985 by winning the British Olivetti Tournament in May. In Vale do Lobo she took third place; and in September 1985 she capped an impressive season by becoming the 415/Vantage European Matchplay Champion. Jane finally finished second in the Merit lists in 1985, after a season-long battle with Laura Davies for first place – in fact, she was just £303 short of taking the title!

Attachment: Royal Musselburgh GC
Sponsor representation: Ben Sayers
Born: February 25, 1964
Birthplace: Haddington, East Lothian
Turned professional: 1984
Tournaments entered: 17
Top ten finishes: 9
Best performances: 1st British Olivetti Tournament, winner 415/Vantage European Matchplay Championship
Amateur record: British Strokeplay Champion 1982, Scottish Champion 1982, British Girls' Champion 1980, Australian Girls' Champion 1982, Scottish Girls' Champion 1978, 79, 80, Scottish Girls' Strokeplay Champion 1978, 80, Curtis Cup 1980, World Cup 1980, 82, World Team Championship 1980, 82, Vagliano Trophy 1981, 83, Scottish international 1979-83
Hobbies: Reading, collecting first editions

Year	Order of Merit	Prize money
1984	8	£8,957
1985	2	£21,234

Tour victories:
1984 Colt Cars Jersey Open Championship, Royal Jersey
1985 British Olivetti Tournament, Moor Hall
1985 415/Vantage European Matchplay Championship, Bramhall

3. Beverly Huke

Beverly, a former LPGA card holder, had her best ever season in Europe in 1985. She finished in third place in the Merit lists for the second time in three years, establishing herself as one of the most consistent players on the tour. Early in the season, she was runner-up to Dale Reid in Ulster; later, in Madrid, she took the Trusthouse Forte Ladies' Classic in an exciting finish

Attachment: Woburn Country Club
Sponsor representation: none
Born: May 10, 1951
Birthplace: Great Yarmouth
Turned professional: 1978
Tournaments entered: 20
Top ten finishes: 12
Best performance: 1st Trusthouse Forte Ladies' Classic
Amateur record: English Champion 1975, British Championship runner-up 1971, Curtis Cup 1972, Vagliano Trophy 1971, 73, 75
Hobbies: Travel, food, music, politics

Year	Order of Merit	Prize money
1979	25	£2,092
1980	30	£935
1981	16	£2,512
1982	19	£1,455
1983	3	£9,226
1984	4	£10,853
1985	3	£18,702

Tour victories:
1979 Carlsberg tournament, Ballater
1980 Carlsberg tournament, Blairgowrie
1983 White Horse Whisky Challenge, Selsdon Park
1983 Playford Classic (joint 1st), Lark Valley
1984 LBS German Open, Braunfels
1985 Trusthouse Forte Ladies' Classic, Madrid

4. Muriel Thomson

In 1985, Muriel again finished in the top ten in the Merit order – continuing her outstanding record of never being out of the top ten! The season started on a high note, despite losing to Gillian Stewart in a sudden death play-off in the Ford Ladies' Classic – and this after scoring a disastrous opening 78! After finishing second to fellow Scot Dale Reid, in the Brend Hotels International, and just when it was looking as though she would not be adding a tour victory to her impressive list, she took the Laing Ladies' Classic by a shot from Vanessa Marvin in October 1985.

Attachment: Murcar GC
Sponsor representation: Marcliffe Hotel
Turned professional: 1979
Tournaments entered: 19
Top ten finishes: 10
Best performance: 1st Laing Ladies' Classic
Amateur record: Scottish Girls' Champion 1973, North of Scotland Champion 1973, 74, Curtis Cup 1978, GB and I World Cup 1978
Hobbies: Skiing, home decorating, Trivial Pursuit

Year	Order of Merit	Prize money
1979	6	£3,043
1980	1	£8,008
1981	3	£8,143
1982	3	£5,529
1983	1	£8,900
1984	9	£8,519
1985	4	£18,631

Tour victories:
1980 Carlsberg tournament, Tyrrells Wood
1980 Viscount Double Glazing, Royal Portrush
1980 Barnham Broom tournament, Barnham Broom
1981 Elizabeth Ann Classic, Pannal
1984 Guernsey Open Championship, Royal Guernsey
1984 Sands International, Saunton
1985 Laing Ladies' Classic, Stoke Poges

5. Debbie Dowling

Despite a slow start to the 1985 season, Debbie went on to win the Vale do Lobo Portuguese Ladies' Open in June. She followed that in the same month with a second place in the Bowring Birmingham Ladies' Classic. Later in the season, she was a finalist in the 415/Vantage European Matchplay Championship, but lost to Jane Connachan. 1985 was the season in which Debbie gained her highest Merit placing to date: she had ten top ten finishes and her total prize money was double that of her previous best.

Attachment: none
Sponsor representation: Dave O'Keele & Co Ltd
Born: July 26, 1962
Turned professional: 1981
Tournaments entered: 20
Top ten finishes: 10
Best performance: 1st Vale do Lobo Portuguese Ladies' Open
Amateur record: Surrey Champion 1980, England international

Year	Order of Merit	Prize money
1981	33	£955
1982	12	£3,187
1983	8	£5,505
1984	14	£7,486
1985	5	£18,097

Tour victories:
1983 Colt Cars Jersey Open, Royal Jersey
1983 Woodhall Hills tournament, Woodhall Hills
1985 Vale do Lobo Portuguese Ladies' Open

6. Dale Reid

After topping the Merit table in impressive style in 1984, it seemed almost inevitable that the talented Scot would suffer something of an anticlimax in 1985. Nevertheless, she finished in the top ten no less than nine times and added two more tour victories to her remarkable record, despite dropping five places in the Merit tables and finishing outside the top four for the first time in four years. In the Ulster Volkswagen Classic, Dale fought off all competition – including the rain! – to win by three shots, after scoring under par for all three rounds. She also won the Brend Hotels International by two shots, when a second-round six under par score of 68 put her on the victory trail.

Attachment: Ladybank GC
Sponsor representation: Costain Construction
Turned professional: 1979
Tournaments entered: 20
Top ten finishes: 9
Best performances: 1st Ulster Volkswagen Classic, 1st Brend Hotels International
Amateur record: Scottish international 1978, runner-up French Girls' Championship

Year	Order of Merit	Prize money
1979	43	£50
1980	12	£2,461
1981	4	£7,322
1982	4	£5,358
1983	4	£8,504
1984	1	£28,239
1985	6	£16,223

Tour victories:
1980 Carlsberg tournament, Coventry
1981 Carlsberg tournament, Gleneagles Hotel
1981 Moben Kitchens, Mere
1982 Guernsey Open, Royal Guernsey
1983 United Friendly tournament, Moortown
1983 International Classic, Lilley Brook
1983 Caldy Classic, Caldy
1984 UBM Classic, Arcot Hall
1984 J.S. Bloor Eastleigh Classic, Fleming Park
1985 Ulster Volkswagen Classic, Belvoir Park
1985 Brend Hotels International, Saunton

7. Kitrina Douglas

Although she slipped five places in the Merit lists, Kitrina had reason to feel quite happy with the 1985 season. During her first year as a professional in 1984 she won two tour events; and her 1985 performances confirmed that she is a force to be reckoned with in the professional ranks, living up to her early promise. Kitrina once had the chance of pursuing a career in the theatre, but decided instead to transfer her stage to the fairways of Europe, acting out a major role as one of Britain's top women golfers.

Attachment: Long Ashton GC
Sponsor representation: Estoril Coast
Born: September 6, 1960
Turned professional: 1984
Tournaments entered: 19
Top ten finishes: 6
Best performances: 2nd Vale do Lobo Portuguese Ladies' Open, 2nd Bloor Homes Eastleigh Classic, 2nd Colt Cars Jersey Open
Amateur record: British Champion 1982, Portuguese Champion 1983, Scottish Girls' Strokeplay Champion 1981, Curtis Cup 1982, Vagliano Trophy 1983, Gloucestershire Champion 1980-84

Year	Order of Merit	Prize money
1984	2	£19,900
1985	7	£15,665

Tour victories:
1984 Ford Classic, Woburn
1984 Hoganas Sweden Open, Molle

8. Gillian Stewart

1985, Gillian's first season as a professional, saw her claim no less than ten top ten finishes from only sixteen tournaments. She made an impressive start to the season, winning the first major tournament, the Ford Ladies' Classic, by pipping fellow Scot Muriel Thomson, to the post in a sudden death play-off. Gillian's 1985 performances suggest that she will be a player to watch in 1986; and her decision to turn professional after missing out on a Curtis Cup place was more than justified.

Attachment: none
Sponsor representation: Claremont
Born: October 21, 1958
Birthplace: Inverness, Scotland
Turned professional: 1985
Tournaments entered: 16
Top ten finishes: 10
Best performance: 1st Ford Ladies' Classic
Amateur record: Scottish U-19 Strokeplay Champion 1975, Scottish Girls' international 1975-77, British Girls' Champion 1976, runner-up Scottish U-21 Strokeplay 1978, Northern Counties Champion 1976, 78, 82, North of Scotland Champion 1975, 78, 80, 82, 83, Scottish Women's Champion 1979, 83, 84, runner-up British Championship 1982, runner-up Spanish Championship 1984, Helen Holm Trophy 1981-84, IBM European Ladies' Open Champion 1984, Home international 1979-84, European Team Championships 1979, 81, 83, Great Britain Commonwealth team 1979, 83, Vagliano Trophy 1979, 81, 83, Curtis Cup 1980, 82, World Cup 1982, 84
Hobbies: Tennis, cookery, keeping fit

Year	Order of Merit	Prize money
1985	8	£15,526

Tour victories:
1985 Ford Ladies' Classic, Woburn

9. Catherine Panton

Spending most of the 1984 season in the U.S.A. meant that for the first time in six years Cathy did not win a tour event. But good performances in 1985 more than compensated for this: she claimed two tour victories and won prize money almost doubling her previous all-time record. She won the McEwan's Lager Wirral Caldy Classic by three shots, followed by the Delsjo Open by just one shot in an exciting finish. In only thirteen tour events she achieved six top ten finishes.

Attachment: none
Sponsor representation: John Letters of Scotland
Born: June 4, 1955
Tournaments entered: 13
Top ten finishes: 6
Best performances: 1st McEwan's Lager Wirral Caldy Classic, 1st Delsjo Open
Amateur record: British Champion 1976, GB & I World Cup 1976, Scottish Girls' Champion 1969

Year	Order of Merit	Prize money
1979	1	£2,495
1980	7	£4,632
1981	2	£8,410
1982	5	£5,137
1983	14	£7,136
1984	31	£2,923
1985	9	£15,029

Tour victories:
1979 State Express tournament, Royal Portrush
1979 Carlsberg tournament, Willingdon
1980 Elizabeth Ann Classic, Pannal
1981 Carlsberg tournament, Queens Park
1981 Carlsberg tournament, Moortown
1982 Moben Kitchens tournament, Mere
1983 Smirnoff Irish Open, Portstewart
1983 UBM Northern Classic, Arcot Hall
1983 Dunham Forest tournament, Dunham Forest
1985 McEwan's Lager Wirral Caldy Classic, Caldy
1985 Delsjo Open, Delsjo, Gothenburg

10. Marie Wennersten *(Sweden)*

Super-Swede Marie had a great 1985, her first season as a professional. She not only won her first WPGA tournament but also finally won her season-long battle with fellow Swede Liselotte Neuman, to become the top non-British player in the Order of Merit. In a closely-fought contest, she managed to beat former Rookie of the Year Kitrina Douglas, to take the 1985 Mitsubishi Colt Cars Jersey Open; and she almost pulled off another victory in front of her own fans in the Delsjo Ladies' Open, when she finished second, a shot adrift of Cathy Panton.

Tournaments entered: 14
Top ten finishes: 6
Best performance: 1st Colt Cars Jersey Open

Year	Order of Merit	Prize money
1985	10	£14,921

Tour victories:
1985 Mitsubishi Colt Cars Jersey Open, Royal Jersey

Fashion on the golf course

Women's golf wear should be practical and comfortable – and, if possible, fashionable. Now, when playing golf, it is not always possible to look your very best, particularly when on a windswept European golf course. Any woman who dislikes having a hair out of place should, almost certainly, give up the game of golf.

However, there is no reason why a woman should not look and feel as attractive as possible when playing golf. Clothing manufacturers now realise that women of all ages want well-cut and stylish clothes that are also practical and comfortable on the golf course, but our female forerunners were not so fortunate. The history of golfing women's fashion mirrors the lack of progress made by women in the game over so many years. Fashion in golf can be seen as more than just an interesting subject – in many ways, it is symbolic of women's lack of freedom for the greater part of golf's history.

In the 1890s (about the time when women were leaving putting courses for the greater excitement of full-length courses), the lady golfer wore a long dress with ballooning sleeves, voluminous petticoats, combinations, a tight-laced corset, and even a hat.

Quite simply, the outdoor dress styles of the late nineteenth century – full and flowing – seriously hindered the full swing of the club so necessary to play golf effectively. It is little wonder that women were trapped on the putting courses for so long. Lady golfers had, of course,

Golfing fashions at St Andrews in 1889. Heavy coats, stiff bodices and plumed hats did little to help women's golfing technique, even on the putting course.

Left: Joyce Wethered, playing at Worplesdon in 1926. The comfortable, loose-fitting fashions of this period were especially practical for the golf course.

also to be careful not to reveal an ankle. The emancipated dress for women pioneered by the famed Amelia Bloomer strangely found few followers on the golf courses of Britain.

Consider for a moment trying to play golf in the following articles: every woman wore a corset, which was not only uncomfortable but also radically altered the shape of some women both above and below the waist. Long skirts were a must. Since wind and damp seem to be perennial features on some golf courses, these were highly impractical. They blew in the wind and got very wet in long grass. To combat the disadvantage of such restrictive garments women resorted to some novel and amusing subterfuges.

Before the turn of the century a number of devices were invented which allowed ladies to vary the length of their skirts. The 'harem'pin, for example, was used to shorten skirts while playing and was removed when near the clubhouse. Another ingenious method was a length of elastic worn around the waist which could be dropped to the knees in a high wind. I wonder how many women cursed its inventor as they tried to make their way round a golf course with knees firmly pinned together by a sturdy length of elastic!

For those who resisted such newfangled and revolutionary notions, one could always bind the hem of the skirt with either leather or braid to prevent the damp from creeping up, and to make cleaning easier. To stop summer skirts blowing about immodestly, the hems were threaded with wire to keep them down. Women in the past certainly knew how to handicap themselves!

Voluminous sleeves were pinned down, or tied with an elastic strap. Hats were fastened securely under the chin by elastic, or pinned to heaped piles of hair. Even then, many women had difficulty keeping them on their heads in high winds.

When high starched collars and striped ties were chic, these too were worn on the golf course, so lady golfers who tried to swing a club often suffered from chafed necks! During winter, heavy coats were the order of the day. As can be imagined, these articles of clothing did little to promote a free arm action or a full, flowing swing.

In short, early golfing outfits were impractical, uncomfortable, and quite unsuitable for golf. Only when corsets became less rigid, and skirt hems shorter, did women have a realistic chance of playing the game effectively. In the Twenties,

Left: Trousers were acceptable on the golf course in the 1940s. The toe-peeping, platform shoes so fashionable at the time were, however, less practical for maintaining a good balance.

when free-flowing dresses became commonplace women golfers adopted knitted garments, cloche hats and dropped waistlines and these clothes were more suitable, comfortable and practical for playing the game. By the 1930s women were playing golf in divided skirts and trousers, although trousers were never fully accepted on the golf course until after World War II.

Since then, golfing fashion has tended to mirror the fashion of the day. This was particularly noticeable during the late 1960s and early 1970s, when hot pants and mini skirts made their way on to some courses, much to the disgust of the old guard.

It is only today that well-cut, colour co-ordinated, comfortable golfing wear has really started to make its mark. Whatever you choose to wear on the course, your prime concern should be that your outfit enables you to swing freely. If you can do that, and feel happy in what you are wearing, then you have the best of both worlds!

Right: Kathy Baker, former winner of the US Open and one of the most stylish women golfers today. Her golfing wear successfully combines comfort with casual elegance.

Sunbeam

Getting started

I didn't try to learn how to play the game of golf until after Nick and I separated. When I was accompanying Nick around the world, teaching me how to play golf was the last thing on the agenda. I obviously knew a great deal about golf, about golf courses, and about golfing personalities, but nothing about how to play the game in practice.

My love affair with the game can be traced to one sunny afternoon in early summer when I was visiting my brother. It was he who suggested that we go into a field behind his house and hit a few balls – using some clubs that Nick had given him.

Back-yard beginnings

My brother stuck an umbrella in the ground, and we hit balls towards it. One of my attempts from about 60 yards actually hit the umbrella. I was delighted and began to experience, first hand, the thrill that makes so many people around the world take such pleasure in hitting a little white, orange or yellow object across vast tracts of countryside towards a four and a half inch hole.

I decided golf might be a game I could play, rather than just *watch*, and I talked my brother into accompanying me on a trip to his local golf course the following day.

At the golf club

At Redbourn Golf Club, my confidence abated a little. For an aspiring player, there is something intimidating about a golf club, even though I had been through the gates of many as a privileged spectator. However, at the club professional's shop, we were warmly welcomed by Nick

Right and below: In the beginning, I spent more time looking for the ball in the rough – and on one occasion in a tree – than on the fairway.

Without the tuition of my coach, Nick Meaker, I would never have mastered the basics of golf so efficiently and easily.

Meaker. We explained we were inexperienced players but wanted to try a round of golf. He suggested we try the Par 3 course, which was open to the general public. We hired the necessary implements and made our way to the First Tee.

My first attempt at playing golf was not an unqualified success. Although only on the short Par 3/4 course (so every green should have been reachable with an iron club from the tee), my ball managed to end up in the undergrowth several times. I spent more time in the bushes attempting to find my wayward ball than I did on the fairways or the putting surface.

I did, however, manage to make good contact with the ball a couple of times. The experience was exhilarating and was enough to convince me that golf offered a challenge that just *had* to be taken up. I was determined to try the Par 3 course again in the very near future.

When I returned the clubs, Nick asked about my progress. I detailed my ineptitude but also my enthusiasm. Nick suggested that, if I were really serious about playing golf, a few lessons could be helpful.

I was pleasantly surprised when Nick told me just how much it would cost me to have his undivided attention for a half-hour lesson – as I mentioned before, about the same as it would cost for a driving lesson. I had imagined it would be much more. My other commitments prevented me from taking advantage of his group lessons at a much reduced fee so I decided to go for individual attention. I made an appointment, and in giving my surname had to explain that although I had been involved with the game for a long time, I had never learned to play it. I was gratified when, as we talked enthusiastically about different tournaments and the game in general, I realised I knew more than I thought about playing the game – at least, in theory.

Importance of tuition

Nick explained why he believed tuition was more vital in golf than in other sports. "Unless you learn the very basics in golf – such as how to grip the club correctly – you can find yourself trying very hard and going nowhere, except into the deepest rough at frequent intervals. Unlike tennis or squash, for example, where a certain 'ball playing ability' is vital for you to play the ball well, golf can be played well by just about everyone, of any age, provided the basic rules are followed." I asked about self-taught golfers, thinking of Lee Trevino, who seems to break all the rule of golf, and yet is one of the greatest players in the world.

"I have met a couple," said Nick, "but even they still benefited from having one or two lessons – even after they had become pretty successful players. I have also known quite a few 'natural ball players' who scorned tuition of any sort, and thus made very slow progress at the game. They had a natural eye, and a swing with a lovely easy rhythm but, although they could play the odd good shot, they still found themselves topping the ball and slicing it all over the place because they didn't know, or more accurately, they hadn't been taught the very basics."

Role of the club professional

I discovered that Nick had flirted with tournament golf, but had, for the time being, decided to concentrate on his duties as a teaching club professional. He talked about his role at the club, and I realised, for perhaps the first time, just how different the lifestyle of a leading tournament golf professional is from that of the full-time club professional.

Both are members of the Professional Golfers' Association, an organisation made up of very fine golfers, and yet the life of a tournament pro is determined by airline schedules and teeing off times, whilst the other is dictated by the opening hours of a club shop and the teaching appointments pencilled in. Both types of professional are essential to the health of the game – although one receives all the accolades. For the other, hopefully, the satisfaction comes from doing a job people thank you for, and the benefits that accrue from a more ordered existence.

Getting started

The following week I arived at Redbourn for my first lesson. When I asked Nick whether I needed to buy any clubs he answered: "No, not just yet. Let's wait and see whether you really enjoy the game before we put you to any expense beyond that which you will be paying for the lessons." I asked how many lessons I would need.

"That varies," said Nick, "but I shouldn't imagine that you'll need more than five or six to get you started. One lesson to learn the very basics, and the others to see if you can then put the basics into practice. I think you'll find there's enough to learn!"

Nick then handed me a single club, slung his well-used golf bag over his shoulder, and gestured towards the door. So began my first lesson.

Lesson 1 - To the practice ground

On the way to the practice ground I was disappointed to learn that I would not be hitting golf balls during my first lesson.

"I think you'll find that you will have quite enough to remember without trying to hit the ball," Nick remarked. "What you are about to learn is, in my opinion, the very essence of the game of golf – how you grip the club and how you address the ball, those vital ingredients which if you don't get right at the very outset can ruin your game, and thus your enjoyment. I'm about to teach you what you should do each and every time you approach a golf ball – and before you attempt to hit it."

I thought it was a good idea to 'address' the ball politely if you wanted it to obey your wishes, but refrained from making this flippant observation. I was, after all, about to make a serious attempt to learn how to play the game about which I knew so much, but understood so little. I asked Nick what he meant by 'addressing' the ball. I was politely told that I was about to find out.

He insisted that I concentrate my attention on what he was about to teach me, and not on how well or badly I might fare during my first lesson. He added, "If you can learn and inwardly digest all that I am about to tell you, and then translate the theory into practice, I'll soon have you hitting the ball down the middle of the fairway." That was, of course, what I wanted to hear. It was also what I wanted to achieve during my first lesson, but not being allowed to show my 'prowess' at striking the ball was frustrating. However, Nick was right, and I found that I had more than enough to digest without trying to hit the ball.

When we reached the practice ground, Nick steered me to an area far away from the other practising golfers.

He explained. "When you come down here to practise by yourself – as I hope you will – remember that you must never practise in front of the line of other golfers, because no matter how far you think you are from them, you'll rapidly discover that some people can produce shots that virtually fly at right angles from their club." I looked at the other golfers in the dis-

Parts of the 7 iron club. Toe of the clubhead. Shots hit out of the toe will fly off line.

Heel of the clubhead. Shots hit from the heel will also fly off line.

tance, thinking Nick was being over-cautious. Later, I discovered that I, myself, was more than capable of some fairly extraordinary right angle deliveries!

Nick asked me for my solitary club: "This is what we call a 7 iron," he said. "Don't worry for the moment why it is called a 7 iron or what its particular job is – apart, of course, for hitting the ball with." I asked why I was given a 7 iron rather than a 3 iron or a 9 iron. "Quite simply," Nick replied, "because I consider it to be the easiest club in the bag to use!"

Nick then continued. "As I instruct you," he said, "I will be asking you to make sure that the leading edge of the club is square to the target – or that the toe of the club is on the ground and not in the air. If you don't know the basic terminology, then it will obviously take me a lot longer to teach you the essentials of the game."

Nick then proceeded to acquaint me with some golf terminology, to make the teaching process easier. I learnt about the toe of the golf club, the heel, the face, the front leading edge, the hosel, the shaft, the grip, and the butt end.

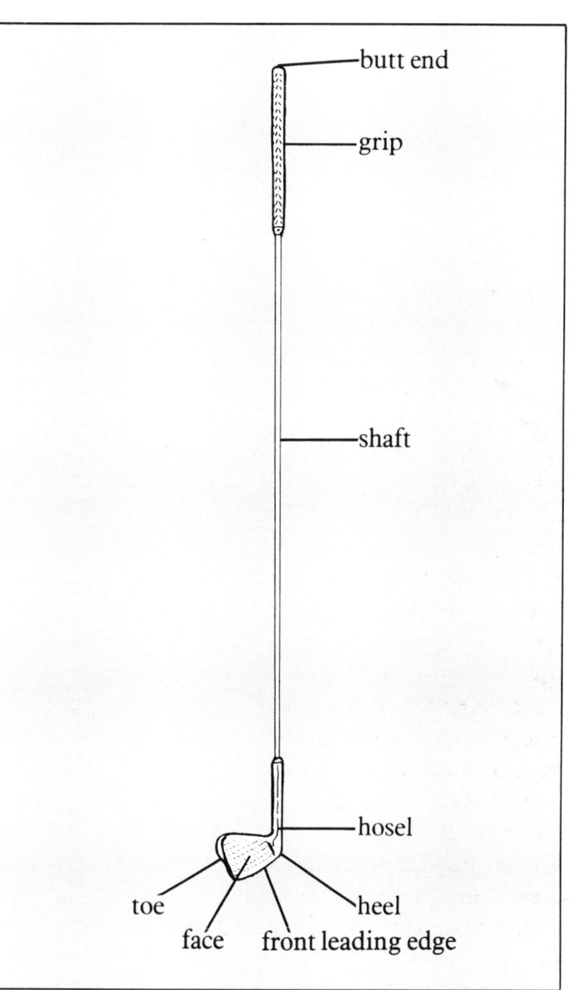

Front leading edge of the clubhead. In the alignment, the front leading edge should be square to the target.

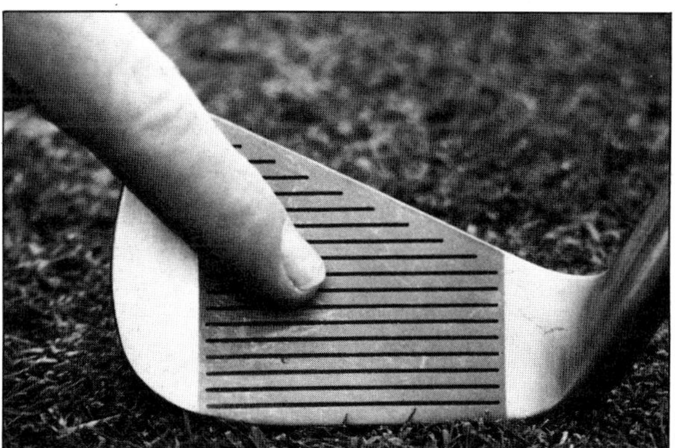

Face or **sweetspot** of the clubhead. Shots hit from the centre of the face should fly straight to the target.

1

2

3

Club at the address position

1. An open clubface at the address position will cause the ball to fly to the right.

2. A closed clubface will cause the ball to fly to the left.

Nick drilled me on the names of the different parts of an iron club and continued testing me until I could remember the difference. We then moved on the the next stage.

Aiming the club

"The next thing I want you to learn," said Nick, "is now to aim the golf club correctly at the target." I replied that surely you just aim the club in the direction of the hole.

"Yes," said Nick, "but you'd be surprised just how many regular golfers forget to aim their club correctly, or think that they have aimed the club – with disastrous results. There is nothing more frustrating than to make perfect contact with the ball only to discover with horror that you've aimed the club incorrectly, and that your ball, rather than sailing down the middle of the fairway, disappears into the thickest rough. To aim the golf club, first place the club behind the ball with the front leading edge square to the target. Make sure that you line up with the front leading edge of the club and not the top of the face. Also make sure that the club is lying *flat on the ground*, with neither the toe of the club or its heel in the air."

Nick asked me to 'aim' the club at the target, a flag seemingly miles down the practice range. This I found more troublesome than I'd expected. First of all, what I thought was 'square to the target' was, in Nick's opinion, far from square. I also had some difficulty making sure that neither the heel nor the toe of the club was 'in the air'.

It took me some time to master this most basic

3. This illustrates the correct alignment of the clubface to the ball at the address position. Always check that the clubface is square when setting up.

stage. Finally Nick agreed that I was capable of aiming the club with a fair degree of certainty and we progressed on to the next stage, how to grip the club.

How to grip a golf club

"The grip," said Nick, "is perhaps the single most important aspect to get right before you start playing golf. The reason we came down to the practice ground without any balls to hit is because it will take me at least a full lesson to explain, firstly, how you should grip the club, and, secondly, how you should address the ball. Most people find this the boring part of the game of golf. However, it is vital to get the basics right before you start learning to hit the ball."

"Is the grip that important?" I asked. "Surely how you swing the club is far more important than how you grip the club?"

"How you grip the club will affect your golf swing and determine how far you are likely to hit the ball and in what direction. You can have the most beautiful swing in the world, but unless you are gripping the club correctly, you will not hit the ball any real distance or in the right direction with any regularity. To play the game of golf well, you have to do everything correctly. A golfer's ability to hit the ball is dependent, firstly, upon the grip and the set-up (how you address the ball) – and secondly, the swing. Believe me, how you grip the club is vital – perhaps the most important thing you'll ever learn about golf."

I soon learned that something as apparently simple as gripping a golf club was, in fact, a precise art. "Lay the grip of the golf club across the face of the left fingers, with the little finger at least half an inch from the butt end. Then close your hand and grip the club with the index and second fingers. Your thumb should be placed down the right side of the shaft. If you are gripping correctly with your left hand, you should be able to see – looking straight down the shaft – only two knuckles of your left hand, and the 'V' formed between the thumb and your index finger should point between your chin and your right shoulder."

I could not see any knuckles. "Then your grip is too weak," said Nick, "and you will probably slice the ball. If, however, you can see more than two knuckles, then your grip will be too strong, and you will probably hook the ball."

I had heard all about infamous 'hooks' and 'slices', but I had never realised that they were caused by the grip. Nick continued, "It's difficult to separate one aspect of a golf swing from another, and both hooks and slices can be caused by a variety of reasons. Golf is very much a game of cause and effect, and if your grip is not correct then you get a whole host of unwanted effects – like the slice and the hook."

I asked exactly what happens when you slice or hook a golf ball. "A slice," Nick explained, "is when the ball (if you are right-handed) literally 'slices' away to the right in an uncontrollable curve. This is caused by the club head imparting a heavy spin on the ball at the point of impact, and it is this spin which causes the ball to slice away. A hook is caused when the opposite spin is imparted on the ball at the point of impact. This spin causes the ball to 'hook' away to the left – again in a horribly uncontrolled curve. We will be looking at exactly what happens when you slice or hook a ball in a later lesson. For the time being, just remember that whoever hooks or slices the ball is likely to spend a great deal of their round looking for their ball in deep undergrowth or woodland. So, pay attention to your grip, and you'll save yourself a lot of trouble and expense!"

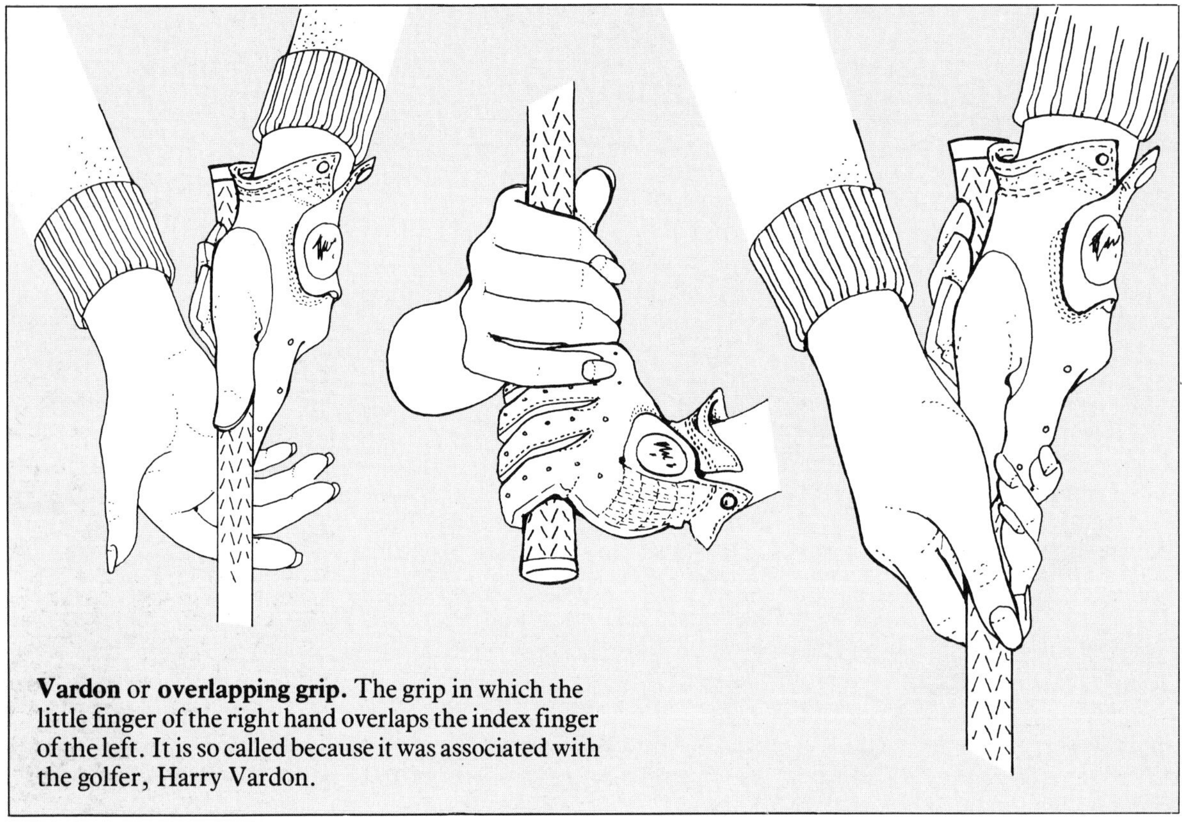

Vardon or **overlapping grip.** The grip in which the little finger of the right hand overlaps the index finger of the left. It is so called because it was associated with the golfer, Harry Vardon.

I asked Nick to check my left hand's grip on the club as my attempts to keep the correct position were causing it to ache terribly. "That's because you are gripping the club too tightly," said Nick. "Let's get your right hand into the action before I explain just how tightly you should grip a golf club. Your left hand grip is now fine – notice how the 'V' formed between your right thumb and your index finger points between your chin and your right shoulder – which is exactly where it should.

"Now place your right hand on the club. I want your hands to work together, and to achieve this, I want you to lay the little finger of your right hand in the depression made between the first and second fingers of your left hand under the grip of the club, and then lay your right hand over the left so that you form another 'V' – which points towards your right shoulder. The three fingers on the grip should exert the pressure."

I did not understand how my hands could work together. Nick went on to explain: "When I say 'hands', I really mean 'hands and wrists'. Just as two hinges have to be in perfect alignment if a door is to swing smoothly, so your wrists need to work together to produce an effective golf swing. They should not fight against each other, as is often the case if your grip is not correct. It is the speed which your hands generate in a golf swing which helps you to hit a golf ball any distance. You can only generate that hand speed if your grip is correct – and your hands and wrists are working together."

He pointed out that my grip was not quite right. "Your right hand is too much underneath the shaft of the club. Move it round a little so that the back of your right hand is facing away from the hole, and not down at the grass. The back of your left hand should face the hole, and the back of your right hand directly the opposite. That is a

Interlocking grip
Place your left hand on the grip of the club, laying the palm of your hand diagonally across the grip. Close your fingers around the grip. The last three fingers should have firm control of the club. Your thumb should lie down the right side of the grip of the club.

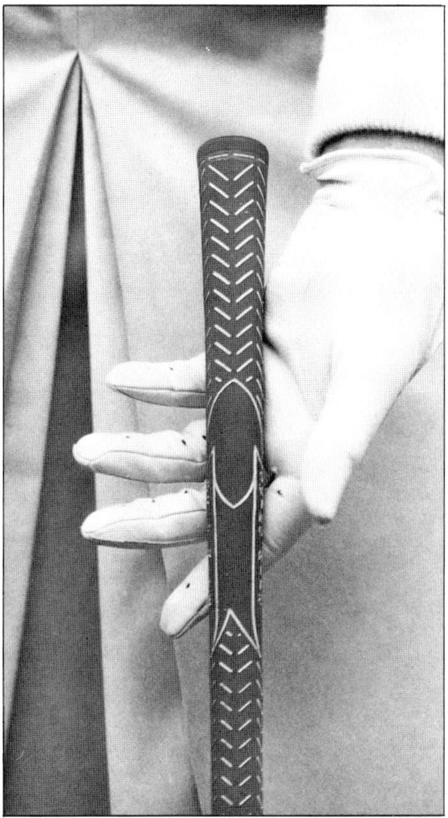

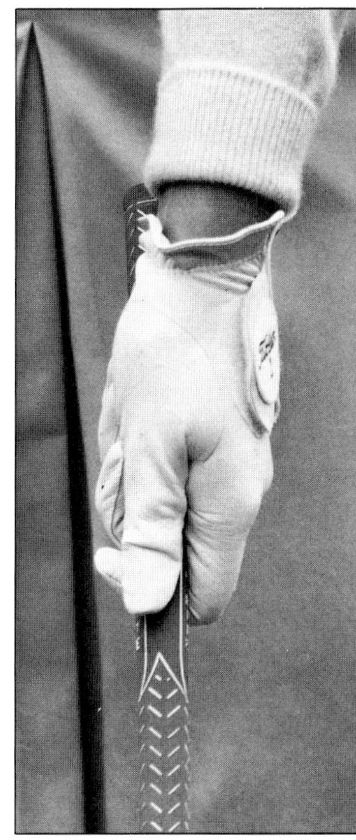

good grip," he said, wrenching my hands into a formation which felt uncomfortable and weak. "Horrible it may feel," continued Nick, "but believe me it is right. If you can persevere with that grip, your muscles will soon adapt and it will rapidly feel much more comfortable."

Vardon and interlocking grips

I asked if there was no other way I could hold the club. "There are two other grips that have been successfully used by top golfers, but the vast majority use the grip I have just shown you – which we call the Vardon grip," Nick answered. I wanted to try the others because I felt I could not hit a thing with the Vardon grip.

"I'll show you one other grip," said Nick, "which we call the 'interlocking grip'. This grip is not used by many great golfers, but it is used by perhaps the greatest – Jack Nicklaus!"

I quite liked the idea of having the same grip as the great Nicklaus. "It's not that very different from the Vardon grip," said Nick. "The only difference is that instead of laying the little finger of the right hand over the depression made between the first and second fingers of your left hand, you interlock the little finger of the right and the index finger of the left hand, like so." He demonstrated, I tried it, and my grip immediately felt stronger.

"It feels much better because your right hand has crept underneath the shaft of the club again," said Nick, as he rearranged my hands once more into the correct position. It still felt much stronger and I begged to be able to use it. "If you really believe it is the grip for you, then use it," said Nick. "Golf is very much a matter of confidence. If you feel more confident using the interlocking grip, then do so. But remember, whatever your fingers are doing, your hands must still be in the correct position – with the 'V'

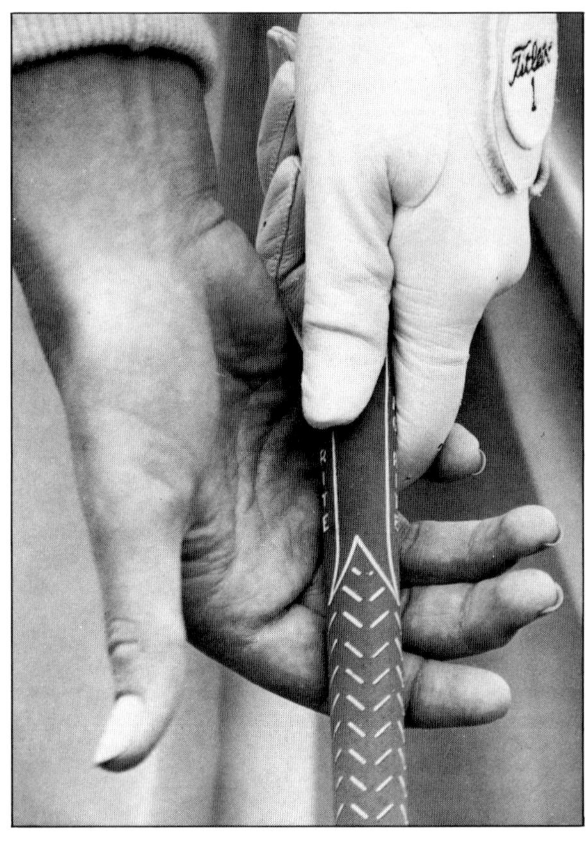

Interlocking grip (cont.)
Place your right hand on the grip so that the palm faces the target. Interlock the little finger of your right hand with the index finger of your left. Your right thumb should lie down the left side of the grip of the club.

made by your two hands as they overlap pointing towards your right shoulder. I personally much prefer the overlapping Vardon grip, but, if your hands are small, the interlocking can feel more comfortable."

This grip really felt far from comfortable, even with my fingers interlocking. Were my thumbs in the right position? Nick assured me that they were. "The thumb on your left hand should be just down the right hand side of the grip, and the thumb on your right hand just down the left hand side of the grip. There is a temptation to place both your thumbs straight down the centre of the shaft – but if you do this you'll find that you won't be able to see the necessary two knuckles of the left hand. The 'V' your hands make will point more towards your chin rather than your right shoulder. Your grip is now perfect, except that, judging by your white knuckles, you are gripping much too tightly."

Thankful to be relaxing my grip, I asked how hard I should grip the club. Nick responded, "If you grip the club too tightly, not only do your hands start to ache fairly rapidly, but you are also likely to be much too tense, with the result that your hands won't work properly. Remember that your grip pressure should come from the first two fingers of your left hand and the pad on top, and from the first three fingers of the right hand. How hard should you grip? Well, imagine that you were about to walk a young child across a busy road. You wouldn't hold the child's hand so gently that he or she could pull it out, nor would you hold it so tightly that it squeals in agony. Just imagine that your golf club is a child's hand."

Nick then instructed me to put my club on the ground, pick it up, aim it at the target, and grip it correctly. To my astonishment, I was able to do it. Now I was ready to learn the 'Set up'.

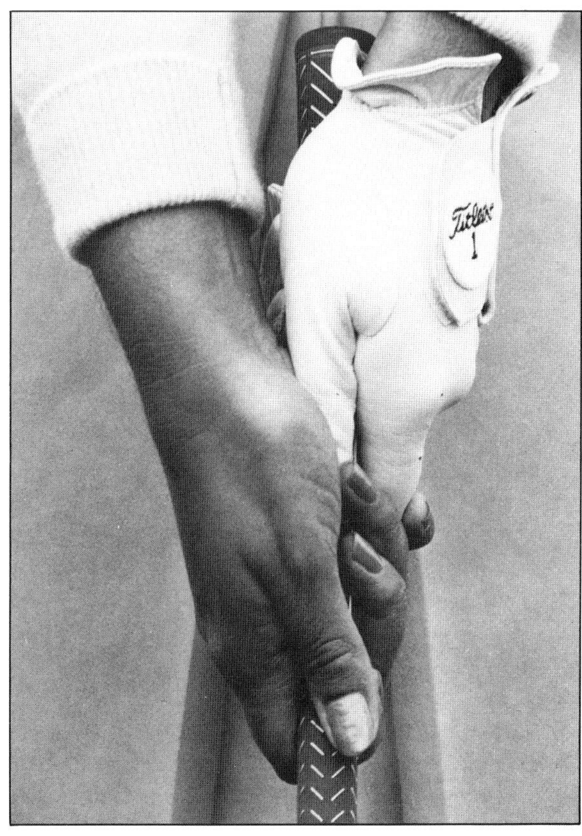

The set-up

"I'm now going to teach you how to stand to the golf ball," said Nick. "I would like you to do this every time you are about to hit a shot. If you can discipline yourself to stand to the golf ball, to go through a routine, then there is a far greater chance that you will 'set yourself up' correctly – and thus hit the ball where you want it to go. So many golfers hit one superb shot straight down the middle of the fairway, charge after it in an enthusiastic frenzy, and then top their next shot and send it dribbling 30 yards into a fairway bunker. They then complain that they can't understand it, particularly after the superb shot they've just hit. The reason for their failure to repeat their brilliant shot is, more than likely, that they rushed their next – and forgot to go through their grip and set-up routine."

Obviously the set-up was another vital ingredient. "It certainly is," Nick confirmed. "As with the grip – if you can get your set-up correct, and remember to repeat it each and every time you address a golf ball – then you'll really enjoy your golf. And, as a result, your game will improve dramatically and rapidly."

Nick continued, "Before you hit any shot, stand behind your ball and 'see' in your mind's eye exactly where you want your ball to go. Then pick a mark just in front of your ball to help your aim. Then aim your club at the target, make sure that the grip of your left hand is correct, and make sure that your left arm is extended comfortably away from your left thigh – about three or four inches."

Distance from the ball

I asked how far I should be standing from the ball. "The club you are using will dictate that distance," said Nick. "Here you are using a 7 iron – which means that you will be standing

1
2

Addressing the ball *(inset pictures)*. When addressing the ball, follow this sequence:
1. With your feet together, lay the grip of your club just above the left knee. This shows the correct distance to stand from the ball.
2. Lift up your hands to create enough space for you to swing the golf club.

much nearer to the ball than you would be if you were using a wood or a 3 or 4 iron, as they have longer shafts. One way to determine how far away from the ball you should be standing is to follow this sequence: 1. Aim your club at the target; 2. Put your feet together; 3. Let the grip of the club drop towards you; 4. Move backwards or forwards until the butt end of the club rests just above your left knee; 5. Bring the club up – and you should find that you have created that comfortable space of about three or four inches between your hands and your left thigh."

I followed Nick's instructions and found that there was indeed about three or four inches space between my hands and my left thigh. I felt encouraged. "Once you have created the space necessary to swing the club clear of the body, open your feet to shoulder width," said Nick. "If I place a club across your toes, that club should be pointing directly at the target." "But where should the ball be?" I asked. "Lined up with my front foot, my back foot, or somewhere in the middle?" "When you are using an iron club," said Nick, "the ball should be in the middle of the stance. Some people say that the ball should always be nearer to the front foot, but I believe that, for iron shots, the ball is better placed in the middle of the stance. When you are using a wood, as you'll later discover, then you tee up the ball much nearer to the front foot."

A balanced stance

I tried as instructed and asked how I was doing. "You are a bit stiff-legged," he replied. "Try and flex them a little. Imagine you are skiing, and remember what happens to those who try to ski with stiff legs! I want to see you look like you are prepared for action, but not about to dive into a freezing lake."

I relaxed – and Nick pointed out another fault. He walked up to me and pushed my forehead. I nearly toppled over backwards. "Balance is also an important part of the set-up. You were resting far too much back on your haunches. Try to distribute your weight evenly. What we are looking for is a perfectly balanced stance." I shifted my weight and almost fell forwards. "Too much on your toes now," he declared. "Try and imagine that all the weight of your body is being pushed down through the arch of your feet."

The tip did help. My stance felt much more secure and Nick agreed. "That's a much better-looking stance. Now you're ready to learn how to swing your club. But before doing so, we'll run through everything I've taught you so far. I want you to take your club from the bag and go through the procedures you've just learned." I concentrated very hard and ran through the sequence:

* Aim the front leading edge square to the target and the ball
* Grip the club correctly
* Body alignment
* Stance
* Check ball position
* Relaxed posture.

My first lesson was over. I had been so engrossed with experiencing golf as a player rather than a spectator that I had not noticed the time passing.

On the way back from the practice ground, I learned that in my next lesson I would be taught the first elements of the swing. "It is no bad thing that the lesson has ended without you attempting the swing," Nick commented, "because you can

Body alignment *(main picture)*. The two clubs show how your body should be square to the target. It is also important to maintain a relaxed set-up.

Lesson 1

Nick explains the correct address position: the feet are open to about shoulder width, the arms are relaxed and the ball is placed in the middle of the stance.

The set-up

It is vital to set up correctly: a proper set-up will enable you to make a good shot even if your swing is not perfect. However, always remember that a poor set-up will result in a bad shot even if you have a good swing. Read the points highlighted in the sections covering **aim**, **grip**, **ball position**, **stance**, **alignment** and **posture** and always follow a careful routine when setting up.

Aim

1. Mentally mark out the ball-to-target line from behind the ball.
2. Choose a point a few feet ahead of the ball on that line.
3. Place the clubhead on the ground squarely, with the shaft positioned at right angles to the intended line of play.

Grip

There are three ways of gripping the club: the Vardon or overlapping grip; the interlocking grip and the baseball or two-handed grip. The interlocking grip is usually favoured by women or golfers with small hands.

Vardon or overlapping grip

1. Place your left hand on the grip of the club, laying the palm of your hand diagonally across the grip.
2. Close your left hand around the grip. The last three fingers should have firm control of the club.
3. Your thumb should lie down the right side of the grip of the club.
4. Place your right hand on the grip so that the palm faces the target.
5. Close your right hand over the grip, overlapping the little finger of your right hand with the index finger of your left.
6. Your thumb should lie down the left side of the grip of the club.
7. The grip of the club should lie across the base of the two middle fingers of your right hand and control of the club should be felt with these fingers.
8. Ensure that the first two knuckles of your left hand are visible and that the 'V's formed by the thumb and the index finger of each hand are pointing towards your chin and right shoulder. If the 'V's point in a different direction your grip is wrong and should be adjusted.

Interlocking grip

Follow the procedure set out above: however, interlock the little finger of your right hand with the index finger of your left.

Baseball or two-handed grip

Place both of your hands on the grip close together but do not overlap or interlock your fingers.

Ball position

The position of the ball depends on the club being used:
1. When using your woods and with any teed-up ball, place the ball opposite the inside of your left heel.
2. For clubs with more loft, place the ball towards the middle of your stance.

Stance

1. Your stance should vary according to the club you are using. As a general rule, your feet should be approximately shoulder-width apart. However, if you have particularly wide or narrow shoulders you should gauge the correct width of your stance by taking a normal walking step; you should then stand with your feet the same distance apart when striking the ball.
2. If you are using a wood or a long iron, you should adopt your widest stance.
3. If you are using a lofted club, move your feet closer together by drawing your right foot nearer to your left.

Alignment

1. Always align yourself in relation to the positioned blade of your club.
2. You should imagine a line drawn across your toes which should be parallel to the ball-to-target line.
3. Your stance, including your knees, hips and shoulders, should be square; that is, aligned in a parallel position to the target.
4. You should alter your alignment slightly when using your sand or pitching wedge. Open your stance by turning your body towards the target.

Posture

Good posture is vital to a good swing:
1. Address the ball.
2. Adopt the correct stance. It is important to relax your body, flexing your knees.
3. Balance your weight evenly on both feet.

You should now feel alert and ready to swing the club.

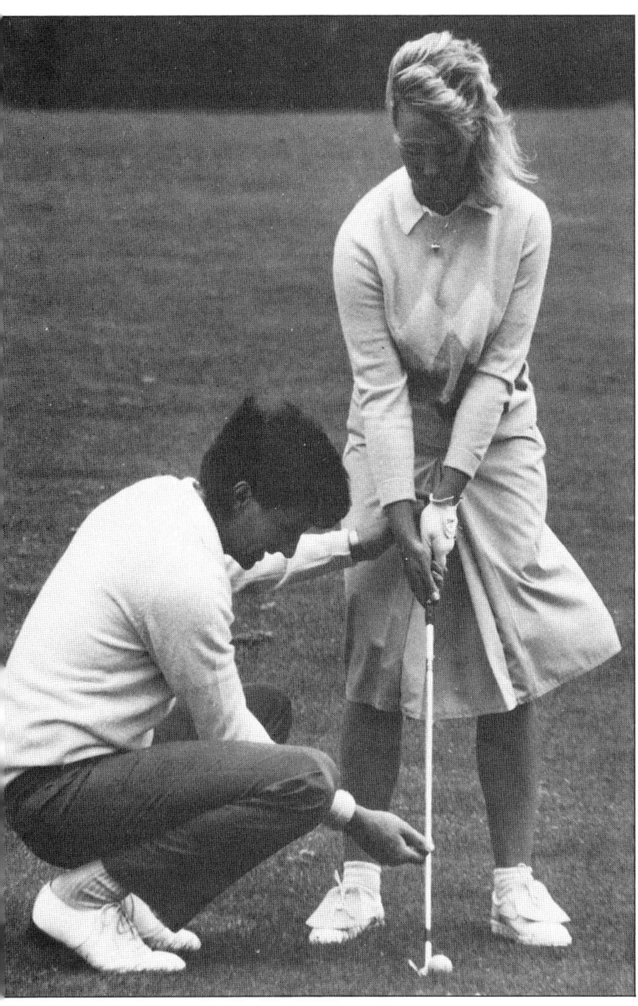

now devote all your time and energy to practising the grip and the set-up, and not being distracted by what most of us find the more enjoyable activity – swinging a golf club."

Practice makes perfect

"If you practise your grip and your set-up in your spare time, and can get into the correct address position without having to think too much about it when you have your next lesson, then I will make much faster progress teaching you how to swing a golf club than I will do if I have to keep reminding you of the basics. I'd like you to hold a golf club as much as possible during the week. For example, try gripping it correctly and holding it out in front of you while you are watching the television. You might also try, again gripping it correctly, scything down a few weeds in your back garden or beating a carpet with it."

I asked, a little sceptically, if such practice would really help me. Nick was insistent. "The more you can acquaint yourself with a golf club and get used to the correct grip, then the better a golfer you will be. It's as simple as that. Try to find the time to practise your set-up. Stand in front of a mirror and make sure that you are aiming the club correctly, that your feet are aligned correctly, and that your shoulders are parallel to the target line." I did not have a club of my own to practise with but Nick held out a battered 7 iron and said I could borrow it until I was sure I wanted to take the game up.

The loan of the club gave me no excuse not to practise. During the week I surprised myself and my friends with my addiction to the battered 7 iron on loan to me. It was my constant companion in the house and garden. I practised on the carpet, among the weeds and in front of my bedroom mirror, running through the set-up procedure time after time. Although I was yet to hit anything vaguely resembling a golf shot, I was hooked and could not wait for my next lesson.

Lesson 2 - Into the swing

"You've learnt the difficult bit," said Nick on the way to the practice ground. "All you've now got to do is hit the ball. If you have mastered the grip and the set-up, then you've already got 60 per cent of the game in the bag. The other 40 per cent – hitting the ball – can cause some problems; and so can the grip and set-up, even though you think you've mastered them." I, however, was determined to show my prowess at the grip and set-up as Nick placed a ball on the scarred turf of the practice range and asked me to address it. My target was a chair which, for some inexplicable reason, was sitting in splendid isolation in the middle of the practice ground.

I ran through the sequence I had practised so often during the week – and to my delight, Nick nodded in approval. "Excellent! You really have got that mastered," he said. "But you're gripping the club a little too tightly, and that is making your arms too tense. Before we move into the swing I'd like to see you a little more relaxed. Not sloppy, but relaxed." I relaxed, and Nick started to teach me the artistry of the golf swing.

The half swing

"I'm going to start you with just a half swing," he said, "because I want you to gain confidence in hitting the ball. I'm not at all worried about how hard or how far you hit it. I'm much more interested in your ability to hit the ball cleanly and with confidence. To help you do this, I'm afraid I'm going to take the ball away for a while – even though I know how keen you are to belt the cover off it."

I wanted to know if there was any good reason for starting with the half swing – apart from it helping to build confidence. "I believe there is," said Nick. "What we want to achieve in a golf swing can, perhaps, best be described as *smoothness*. You don't 'hit' a golf ball, you stroke it away with controlled power – and this controlled power comes more from rhythm and timing than naked aggression and brute strength. I want you to swing smoothly, and believe that the best way I can show you just how effective such a swing can be is by you giving a demonstration.

"What happens during the first eighteen inches of your backswing determines, to a great extent, what happens to your swing from that point onwards. I want you to concentrate on the first eighteen inches of your swing, and, for the time being, don't worry about what is happening to your club at the top of your backswing. As I told you during your first lesson, it's vital that your hands and wrists work together during your golf swing – it is their speed which dictates, to a great extent, just how far you will hit the ball. To make sure that you understand and feel what it means to 'make your hands work', I'm going to teach you an exercise called 'stroking the grass'."

Stroking the grass

I got into the set-up position once again, and Nick demonstrated what he meant by 'stroking the grass'. "Before you try to hit the ball using a half swing, try just stroking the grass. I want you to start swinging the club back smoothly keeping your left arm straight, but not rigid. You mustn't lift the club up, but swing it back by turning your shoulders. The start of your swing is, as I've already said, vital. Don't jerk the club back but take it away smoothly."

I was a little puzzled, since I had seen many good golfers swing back very quickly – and said so. But Nick explained, "Remember that the speed of the club head at the time of impact with the ball is all that counts. A person with a fast backswing is likely to have a fast downswing – but the speed of the club head should be at its

Half swing
1. Swing the club back, keeping the left arm straight. The left knee should point at the ball and the shoulders should turn naturally.
2. Swing through the ball and extend the arms towards the target.

1

2

maximum as it strikes the ball – and that isn't always the case with fast swingers. Try and think 'slow' during your swing. Ease the club smoothly away from the address position, keeping your left arm straight, and swing it back until it is parallel to the ground and pointing directly away from your target."

I tried taking the club back smoothly, but found it a little difficult. "If you are gripping the club correctly," said Nick, "which you are, then your hands and club should move away from the address position as one unit. Some people do manage to move their hands away and leave the club head lagging behind, others cock their wrists much too early – with the result that the club head leads their hands. For the first eighteen inches, at least, move your hands and club together. It is only after you have brought the club back on line to this distance that your wrists start to come into play."

I tried the 'take away' and Nick nodded in approval. But I was still uncertain about how far I should take the club back for a half swing, and Nick replied, "As I said, the shaft of the club should be parallel to the ground, and the head of the club should be pointing directly away from the target. When you have reached that height smoothly, then let the club descend naturally. Don't try and 'hit from the top of the swing', but let the club head *accelerate* to the point of impact – which should be where your club was resting before you started your backswing. Let the club swing through and just brush the grass. Try it about 20 or 30 times, and I think you will begin to feel how your wrists come into play – how they work."

I tried 'brushing the grass', but not with much success; my club seemed to insist on caressing the air above the grass. "Your wrists are not working," said Nick, "because your grip is too tight and your left arm is too rigid. Try to relax a little." I did, and soon began to brush the grass with a smooth and satisfying regularity.

Nick interrupted and placed a bright yellow practice ball on the turf. This was the moment I had been waiting for! I was now going to try to hit a golf ball.

Hitting the ball

Nick quickly cautioned me, "Now concentrate. Just because there is now a ball in front of you begging to be hit, don't forget all that I have told you. Remember that the ball isn't going anywhere until you strike it – so there is no hurry."

I went through the sequence I had so carefully learned: I aimed the club square to the target, made sure that my grip was correct, checked my distance from the ball, checked the ball position, checked my alignment, tried to relax, and was about to swing when Nick said, "Give your club a little waggle to free your wrists, and remember to keep your eyes on the ball. Then just imagine that you are brushing the grass – not hitting a golf ball."

I did so and was delighted to hear a satisfying 'clunk'. Looking up, I was thrilled to see the ball soaring away in a graceful loop right down the middle of the practice ground! It was incredible and Nick, too, was impressed. "Tremendous," he said. "Look how far you've hit that ball with only the shortest of swings. That's what timing and rhythm can do for you, and hands that are *working*."

I already had another ball scooped into position and swung, but there was a hollow clipping sound. I looked up to see the ball hip-hopping its way far to the right of my target line. I immediately grabbed another ball, swung, and looked down to see that the ball had not moved an inch. I was about to grab another when Nick said, "Hold on. You are forgetting everything that you've learnt. What did I tell you to do each and every time before you hit a golf ball?" Elated after the first swing, I had forgotten to go through the sequence. Abashed, I took another ball and promised to do it correctly.

I went through the set-up procedure, swung, and the ball soared into the air. The next ball, however, nearly flew off the club face at right angles. "You tried to hit that one much too hard," said Nick. "I know it's difficult, but don't get carried away. Treat each and every golf ball with the same respect, and think slow and smooth. If you get into the habit of thinking about your grip and set-up every time you address a golf ball, then your game will improve dramatically. When you come down here to practise, for example, don't just stand here whacking ball after ball, but think about each shot. It's far better practice to hit twelve balls well, than 120 all over the place. When we get on the golf course you'll find that whoever hits straight, scores low – and that, after all, is the aim of the game!"

I hit a few more balls, making sure I thought about each and every shot, but the lesson was now up, Nick informed me. The time had gone astonishingly quickly and I was excited enough to want to get on with the full swing. I begged Nick to take me for another lesson immediately. "Even if I had the time," said Nick, "I wouldn't give you another lesson now. Although you don't realise it, I can see that you're already getting tired. To learn effectively you need to be fresh,

Practice can be carried out on a driving range. Many are covered and floodlit for use at night.

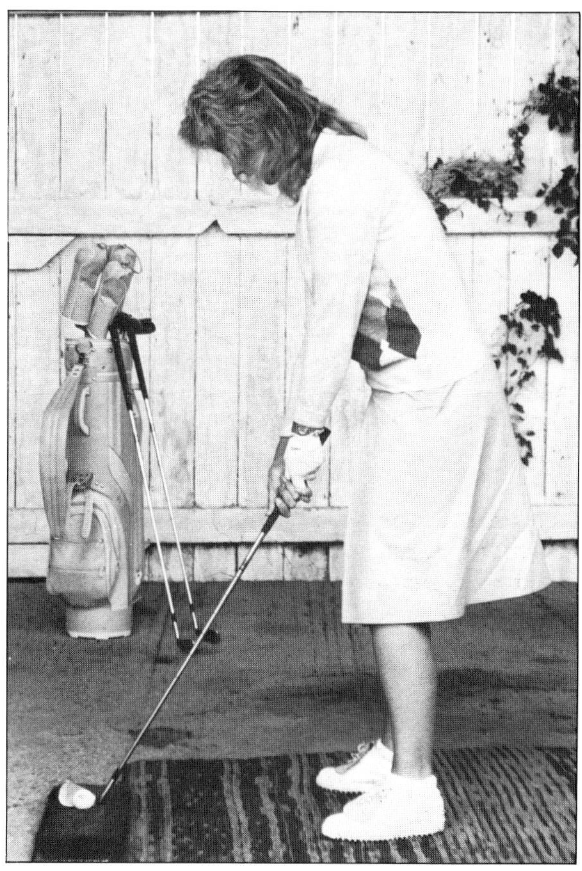

and half-an-hour is quite enough for any beginner. Surely you've got enough to practise before I see you next?"

I had, but I was sure my neighbours would not approve of me hitting even half swings towards their beloved greenhouses. "Practise stroking the grass," said Nick. "It really is an effective exercise. The more you can get your wrists to work in a controlled way, the better a golfer you will be. If you get a little tired of brushing the grass, buy an air ball – which is plastic and full of holes. You'd have to hit that pretty hard to do any damage. Remember, however, that even when you are practising in your back garden, to run through your set-up procedure, keep to your half swing, and don't try and hit the ball too hard."

On the driving range

During the next week I had to restrain myself from rushing off to a driving range to practise. The only thing that held me back was a fear of making a fool of myself in front of other people. But after endless hours practising in the back garden after work, I tired of 'brushing the grass' and hitting bits of mud on the doormat in my front garden. I decided to visit my local golf range. Once there, I paid for a bucket of balls and took a long hard look at my fellow novices. It was obvious that the golf bug strikes all sorts. Golf balls were flying in all directions and at all velocities. Few on the range were taking Nick's advice and 'setting themselves up' before each swing, rather the reverse. It looked like a competition to see who could get rid of their bucket of balls the quickest!

I felt very knowing as I made my way to a spare mat. I carefully went through the grip and set-up procedure for my first three shots, and resisted the temptation to try a full swing. I was rewarded by nicely struck little shots looping gently down the middle. Flushed with success, I decided to hit the ball a little harder, and lengthened my swing – with disastrous results! The ball flew off the toe of the club and nearly decapitated the elderly gentleman who was practising in the next-door booth. I apologised profusely but, instead of slowing down, proceeded to try and dispatch the balls in my bucket as quickly as possible. The results were predictable and I left the driving range both angry and dispirited.

Lesson 3 - The full swing

After my experience at the driving range I felt humiliated and my borrowed and battered 7 iron lay untouched and unloved for two days.

I arrived at Redbourn for my next lesson, no less enthusiastic but less confident, and told Nick about my experience at the driving range. "Well, at least it should have taught you a thing or two," said Nick. "One, that you should only practise what you have been taught and know how to do; and two, that your mental approach to the game can be almost as important as the technical perfection of your swing. When you hit a bad shot, or generally 'make a fool of yourself' in front of others, you mustn't let it affect your next shot. When you are out on the course, one bad shot *should* only result in you dropping one shot, or at most two. If you let it affect you and you get flustered, your game will literally go to pieces. You will drop countless shots and become thoroughly dispirited. Golf is a different game from most you'll encounter in this respect: every time you approach the ball you have another chance. If you can forget the disappointments of a preceding round, then you can still score well – if you keep your control and remember, above all else, to go through your set procedure."

At the practice ground, I ran quickly through all I had learnt on my previous lessons, 'brushing the grass' a few times, and then hitting a dozen or so balls with the half swing. Nick seemed pleased with my execution and began to teach me how to hit a golf ball effectively using a full swing of the club. "With the half swing, you're hitting the ball beautifully crisply. I now want to put a little more power behind your swing, and this we'll achieve not by *hitting harder*, but by swinging *longer*. If you can keep the rhythm you've achieved on your half swing for the full swing, then you'll hit the ball quite some distance without any effort at all," said Nick. He continued, "The full swing is a natural extension of the half swing. You'll find, however, that the full swing can bring some very unwanted elements into your game – most noticeably, a loss of control if you try and hit the ball too hard."

The backswing

"All the essential ingredients of the half swing are even more essential when you graduate to the full swing. You must make absolutely sure that your set-up is correct, and then take the club back smoothly, keeping your left arm straight, but not rigid. During the full swing you'll find that your legs and hips come much more into the action."

I tried to copy the leg action I'd seen employed so effectively by professional golfers. "Don't *consciously* try and do anything with your legs during the backswing," said Nick. "As your shoulders and hips begin to rotate, your legs will naturally do what they should – if you are swinging correctly."

I tried lengthening my backswing but found that this 'natural extension' brought new problems. My left arm, for example, felt uncomfortable.

"That's because you are not turning your shoulders enough or letting your wrists 'break' on your backswing," said Nick. "Your legs and hips also have to come into action and your legs have become much too rigid once again. Relax them a little, turn your shoulders, and you'll see what happens."

I relaxed, swung *smoothly* back, and my left knee moved towards the ball, making it much easier for me to achieve a full shoulder turn. It felt more comfortable and my left arm was straight. "Much better," said Nick, "but you're now dipping your left shoulder towards the ground. You mustn't dip your shoulder, but

1

2

Backswing
1. Nick takes me to the top of the backswing.
2. From the half swing, take the club up, letting the wrist break.

rotate it – trying all the time to keep your head as steady as possible and your eyes firmly on the ball. Your hips should also rotate as your shoulders turn. Don't forget to let your wrists 'break' a little at the top of the swing, and remember that your wrists and hands should be firm, not rigid."

I tried again, and found the movement much more fluid. Nick, however, commented, "Your hips are now swaying, not rotating. Try and turn your body, don't sway back. There's a little exercise we can try here." Nick disappeared into a nearby shed and reappeared carrying two low back chairs. "They're not for sitting on," said Nick, "but to teach you not to sway. Get into your address position, please."

I did as instructed, and Nick placed the two chairs either side of me – one with its seat facing down the practice ground and its back towards me on my left side, and the other with its seat facing the opposite direction and its back towards me on my right. He then asked me to swing, and I found my hips rocking the chair on the backswing. "That's because you're swaying," said Nick. "Try again, and concentrate on turning or coiling those hips, not swaying."

I tried again. The chair on the backswing side didn't move but the chair on the downswing side rocked as my hips encountered it. "You mustn't sway on either the backswing or the downswing if you can possibly help it," said Nick. "Try and imagine that your head is the centre of a wheel, and that you are going to swing your club in a smooth arc around that centre – without the centre moving."

I tried again, with more success, and Nick removed the chairs. However, I was worried about where the club head should be at the top of the backswing. "For the time being, don't worry where the head of your club is," said Nick, "just concentrate on swinging smoothly, keeping your head as steady as possible, and watching the ball. I'll soon tell you if there is something wrong with the position of your club head."

I asked if I was swinging back far enough. "Perfectly far enough," said Nick. "You're swinging back just as far as a full shoulder and hip turn and a nice, straight, firm left arm will allow. If your left arm starts to bend early, then you are not turning your shoulders and rotating your hips sufficiently. The result will be that your legs remain inactive – which, as you know, is not desirable. Remember that leg movement is an *effect* of a good backswing, not a *cause*. If you are getting a good shoulder turn, and coiling your hips effectively, then your legs will do what they should do without you having to tell them. Exaggerated leg movement leads to loss of control."

The downswing

I tried a few swings and concentrated on rotating, not swaying. Nick nodded with approval, then began to talk about the downswing. "The downswing should mirror exactly what you have been doing so effectively when using the half swing. Remember that we want to achieve a smooth, accelerating arc – with maximum speed at the point of impact. Don't, therefore, 'hit from the top'. Let the club swing smoothly down and let your hands and wrists generate the speed.

"The best way to achieve this smooth acceleration is to let your legs lead the downswing. On the backswing, I asked you to forget about what your legs were doing and to concentrate on a smooth take-away and a full shoulder and hip turn. Your legs at the end of the backswing moved naturally into the right position. Your left knee bent in and pointed to a position behind the ball, and your right knee stayed very much in the position it was at the address. Try to remember that you should never lock your right knee straight – as so many beginners do. At the top of your backswing, about 70 per cent of your weight shifts *naturally* on to the outside edge of your right foot, with the rest on the inside edge of the left foot. Your left foot elevates just enough to allow a full and free hip and shoulder turn."

Nick noticed my bemused expression. "Now, I don't want you to *consciously* think about that mass of information as you're swinging the club back *smoothly*. When you have reached the top of your backswing, however, I want you then to think 'legs' – because it is at that moment that they really come consciously into play. All you have to do to start your downswing is shift your weight to your left foot and side. As your weight shifts, then your downswing will begin naturally. Your shoulders will start to unwind and your hips will uncoil."

I needed to know what my hands should be doing. "Keep your hands *leading* ahead of the club and let the club head descend smoothly," said Nick. "It will increase its speed as it swings down and your hands and wrists start to come into action. If your grip is correct, they will do this naturally so, again, don't try to consciously bring your hands into the action. They will return to the position they were at the address as you make contact with the ball. Once you have hit the ball and extended towards the target, they will then 'roll over' to allow you a full follow through."

Nick explained what he meant by 'extended towards the target'. "I'd like you to feel as if you were throwing the club itself at the target. That is what I mean by 'extension'. I don't want to see

The swing action. Move the club away from the ball with your hands and arms, your shoulders turning naturally.

you swinging round your body on either the backswing or the downswing. I want to see a nice flowing arc, with your club hitting right through the ball and then 'extending towards the target'."

"What should my legs be doing during the downswing and follow through?" I asked. Nick replied, "Once you have shifted your weight on to your left foot and side, your legs will then take care of themselves. Just concentrate on watching the ball, swinging right through it, extending your club towards the target and, believe me, your legs will do what they should."

Nick went on. "In fact, once you have transferred your weight to your left side, your right knee 'releases' towards the target. All weight is now on your left side, so it is vital that it remains firm and in control. If your left side collapses or sways forward during your downswing, you will be in trouble. As you swing through the ball, your right heel will elevate as your right knee 'kicks in' to point at the target. At the end of your swing, all the weight will have been transferred to the outside of your left foot – but you should still be able to finish in a balanced position."

I took a full swing but felt slightly unsteady at the end of the follow through. Nick commented, "Swing smoothly and within yourself, and use your right leg to help you balance. I'm not asking you to lift your right leg off the turf, but merely to shift the bulk of your weight on to your left foot. Go back to the half swing for a second."

I did, and Nick pointed out how well balanced I was at its completion. He then took me slowly through to a full follow-through position saying, "That's where you should finish. You're balanced enough now. See if you can take a full swing and finish in as balanced a position.

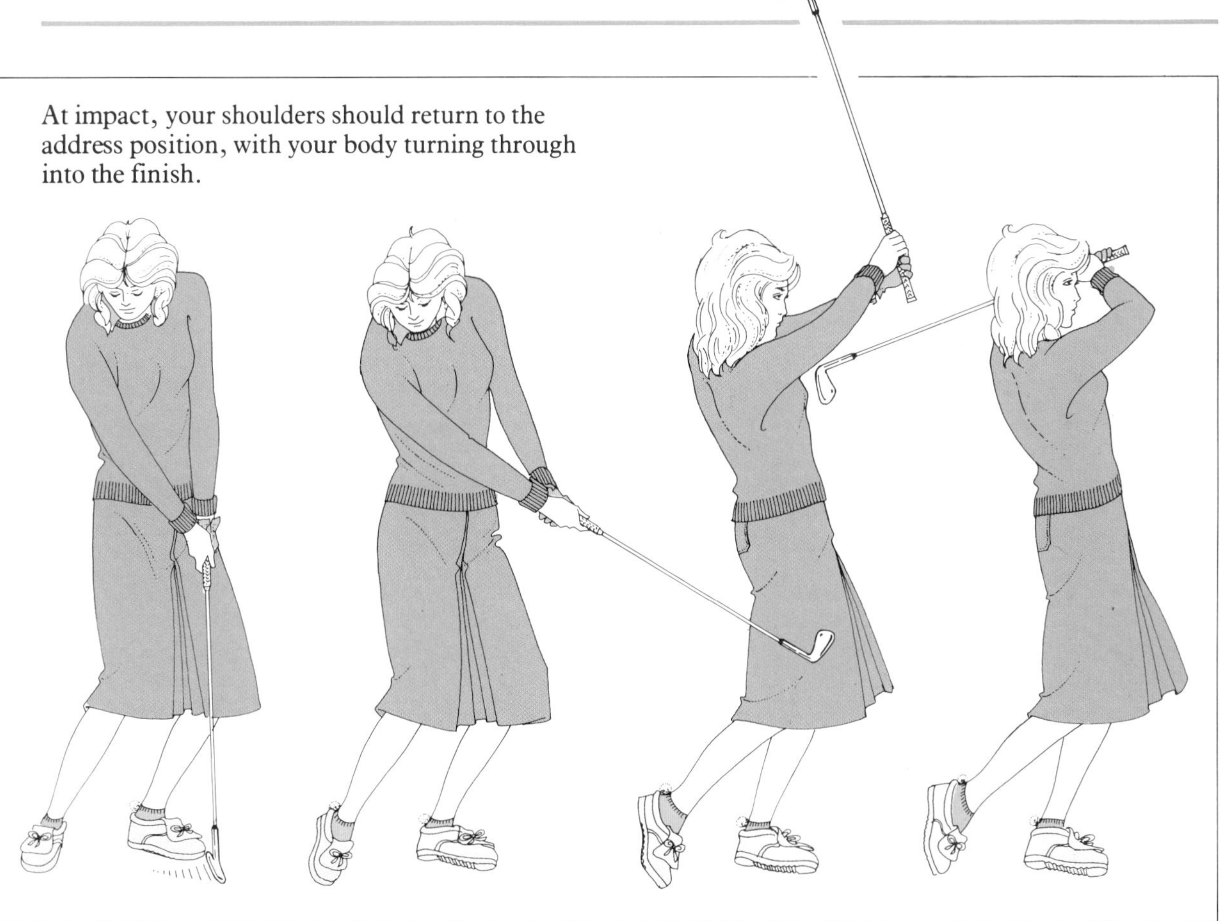
At impact, your shoulders should return to the address position, with your body turning through into the finish.

Remember to swing smoothly and you shouldn't have any trouble." I swung smoothly and, remarkably, ended my follow through perfectly balanced.

After a few more practice swings, Nick made one final point before rolling some balls in my direction. "A good tip is to try and 'aim' your tummy button at the target when you have completed your swing – and remember not to be too eager to see where your ball has (or has not) gone. In other words, don't lift your head too soon! It should stay down much longer than most people imagine. It should release *naturally* as you swing through the ball. Don't jerk it up prematurely or you'll be accused of 'not watching the ball' with reason – and suffer the embarrassing consequences!" I took the point and tried to remember not to lift my head until the ball had left the club.

Nick then placed a ball on the turf and pointed to the flag that was to be my target. "If you hit this ball sweetly," he said, "you should be able to reach that with your 7 iron." I looked at the distant flag and shook my head. Nick chided me, "Be confident. There's no rush. Just go slowly through your set-up procedure, keep a calm and thinking head, swing smoothly, and you might surprise yourself."

Concentrating intently on the little yellow ball in front of me, I painstakingly ran through the complete set-up procedure. I swung smoothly – and the ball hip-hopped away in an embarrassing curve far to the right of its target. I exclaimed in anger and exasperation.

Some common errors

"You swung from 'out to in' and hit the ball with the hosel of your club," said Nick calmly. "Out to in – in to out – and in to in. I didn't want to

1

2

3

Full swing
1. Adopting the correct set-up.
2. The hand, arm and body position at the top of the swing.
3. The follow through with arms extended high so that the clubhead finishes high over the left shoulder.

The swing

You will only perfect your swing with continual practice. Follow these guidelines to enable you to 'groove' your swing:

1. Adopt the correct set-up. Remember to keep your eyes on the ball and your body relaxed throughout the swing.

2. Concentrate on the correct swing path, that is, the path you intend the clubhead to follow.

3. Take the clubhead away from the ball, keeping your arms and wrists as straight as possible. The club should travel on a circular plane to about waist height.

4. As you move through the swing, allow your wrists to break and your hands to become active.

5. The clubhead should travel down on an inside path. Your wrists should now be straight and you should return to your address position as you approach the ball.

6. You should execute a full follow through, extending your arms high so that the clubhead finishes over your left shoulder.

mention such horrors until necessary. Since you've unfortunately brought the subject up, lend me your club and I'll show you what I mean."

Nick placed a ball on the grass, and then laid a club across his feet pointing directly at the target, and another the far side of the ball parallel to the first. "I've laid these tramlines to help you see exactly what I mean by 'in to out' and 'out to in', and what type of bad shots can result from such bad practice," said Nick. He then asked me to stand directly behind him before saying, "The shot you just played could, perhaps, be described as a 'shanked slice'."

Nick reproduced the very shot I had played – first at speed, and then in slow motion – and then explained. "Most people would consider the 'shank' or the 'socket' to be the most horrendous shot in golf. You actually hit that ball out of the heel near the hosel of the club. Your club face was much too open and the ball, after hitting the shank, was swiped away by the club face in a hopping slice.

"To achieve a shot of such horrific dimensions, you first rocked forwards on to your toes as you brought the club back. This, obviously, caused your swing to be out of alignment. You then swung the club 'out' at the top of your backswing (try to remember the wheel – the arc your club took resembled that of a buckled wheel!) and then 'sliced' across the ball causing it to spin away violently. The path your club took on the follow through was 'in' – which means that rather than extending *towards* the hole, your club swung across the ball, and across the target.

"It's perhaps useful if you imagine the ball as the central pivot of the hands of a clock. Your target is 12 o'clock, and you therefore want your club to swing back through 6 o'clock. On the shanked slice you just played, your club went through 4 or 5 o'clock on your backswing and through 10 or 11 o'clock after you made contact with the ball."

"What happens to the ball if I swing 'in to out'?" I asked, fascinated by Nick's review of the horror shots. "Then you'll 'push' the ball out to the right," said Nick. "As I've already explained, a slice imparts a lot of spin on the ball which causes the ball to slice away. When you 'push' the ball, your club actually meets the ball 'square' to the swing path – 'in to out' and the ball flies straight to the right. Your club follows a path from about 7 or 8 o'clock through to somewhere in the region of 1 or 2 o'clock. Normally the push is caused by your alignment which is why it's so important to first aim your club at the target and then align your feet correctly. These

Faults

All golfers have at times experienced problems with the direction of their shots. Listed below are the usual causes of the more common problem shots: reading them may help you to help yourself.

The slice

The slice is a shot that curves away to the right.

Common causes:

1. You will slice the ball if the clubface is too open on impact: make sure that the clubface is square to the target as you hit the ball.

2. You will slice the ball if your wrists are too tense.

3. If your grip is too weak you will slice the ball.

The hook

The hook is a shot that bends to the left.

Common causes:

1. Bad grip: ensure that your right hand is not underneath the club and that your left hand is not too much on top.

2. Rolling your wrists too quickly before hitting the ball.

club tramlines I'm using should help you to align yourself 'square' to the target."

The review of horror shots was not yet complete. Nick went on, "In addition to the push and slice which are caused by swinging 'in to out' and 'out to in' respectively, there is also the 'pull' and the 'hook'. A pull is close cousin to the push and, like the slice, is caused by an 'out to in' swing. Like the push, it is more the result of bad alignment than anything else. The club meets the ball square, but due to faulty alignment, the ball flies away in a straight line far to the left of the target."

Nick continued, "A hook is caused by a swing

Nick demonstrates the in-to-out swing or push, by swinging the club too close to his body and inside the correct swing path.

He is now swinging the club outside the correct swing path on the follow through. This results in a shot that flies to the right of the target.

The shank
The shank is a shot that often occurs when the player is attempting to pitch or chip the ball. It is effectively the result of a mis-hit, when the ball is struck by the part of the club nearest the hosel.
Common causes:
1. Standing too close to the ball.
2. Moving your body weight from your heels to your toes.

Topping
A shot that, not surprisingly, results from a player striking the top of the ball so that it runs along the ground.
Common causes:
1. Too much body tension as you swing.
2. Lifting your head up too soon after playing the shot.
3. Swaying whilst playing the shot.

The push
The push is a shot that flies straight out to the right of the target.
Common causes:
1. Bad alignment.
2. A push may be caused by a swing that is in-to-out through impact; that is, a swing that comes inside or around the body on the take-away and outside the correct swing path on the follow through.
3. Incorrect ball position: if you place the ball too far towards your right foot, this will result in you hitting the ball before your club has reached a straight path.
4. Bad leg work: this may cause the ball to be played off the right foot instead of the left.

The pull
The pull is a shot that flies straight out to the left of the target.
Common causes:
1. Bad alignment.
2. A pull may be caused by a swing that is out-to-in through impact; that is, a swing that moves outside the correct swing path on the take-away and then inside on the follow through.
3. Incorrect ball position: when the ball is placed too far towards the left foot.
4. Allowing the right side of your body to dominate will result in a left-aimed shot. Remember, golf is a game dominated by your left side.

Nick shows the out-to-in swing. His take-away is outside the correct swing path. On the follow through, he pulls into his body hitting across the ball. The result is often a pulled shot, with the ball flying off to the left of the target.

that travels 'in to in' – or from about 7 o'clock to about 11 o'clock. Quite often, this is caused by too flat a swing – one that is more like a baseball swipe or a hockey hit. The club head 'travels' inside its desired path on the backswing, and mirrors this fault on the downswing and follow through. The club face is 'closed' at the point of impact – a fault that is often caused by your hands turning over too quickly."

After this detailed explanation, there was no excuse for me not knowing about the slice and the hook, the push and the pull, and the horrible shank, so when Nick suggested I try another ball, I concentrated hard and remembered about extending towards the hole on the follow through. I went through the set-up meticulously, lined up impeccably, and swung the club. It met the ball with a satisfying clunk – and I extended towards the target on the follow through. My swing brought my head up naturally, I saw my ball sailing through the air towards the target and let out a squeal of delight. The feeling was magical and I instantly wanted to play another ball.

Nick agreed but only on the condition that I take my time. This time I swung the club and the ball hip-hopped and scuttled down the middle. I banged the club against the innocent turf in anger. "You topped it," said Nick. "You tried to hit that one much too hard and *scooped* it away. Let your club lift the ball and let your power come from rhythm and timing, not animal strength. Your hips swayed back on your backswing that time. Remember you mustn't sway, but turn."

I tried again and, after making contact with the ball, took off a lump of turf, jarring my wrist in the process. I flung the club down impatiently and rubbed my tingling wrist. "It may surprise you to hear," said Nick, "that I would consider

The full swing – the exhilaration shows on my face.

that, very nearly, an excellent shot. Your wrists hurt only because the ground is very hard, and your wrists aren't 'golf hardened' as yet. Look where your ball finished." I looked, and saw that it had finished quite some way down the practice ground.

"The only thing slightly wrong with that golf shot was your placement of the ball. It was a little too near your right foot, but only very slightly," said Nick. "Strangely enough, when you use an iron club correctly, you hit *down* in order to get the ball *up*. This isn't something I would normally go into at such an early stage in a golfer's career, but because you nearly hit the 'perfect iron shot', I'll explain. The idea is to hit the ball with the iron club just *before* it reaches the lowest part of its arc. The club therefore hits the ball first and then takes a shallow divot of grass. That is how to play a perfect iron shot, but, for the time being, and particularly since this ground is rock hard, concentrate on hitting the ball cleanly off the turf. You are obviously familiar with the way the professionals take a huge divot when they play their iron shots, and it is, of course, easier to take an impressive divot on the well-watered American courses. When the tournament professionals are playing a rock-hard British Links course they have to adapt – or end their round with very tingling wrists."

Nick suggested I hit five more golf balls before ending the lesson. The first four I hit were so-so, but the last was really magnificent. The ball literally hummed from the club, flew up in a graceful arc, and landed right in the middle of the practice ground. "That's a perfect way to finish," said Nick. "Always quit when you're on top. I've seen too many people hit a beauty, try just one more, and then spend an hour blasting balls all over the place in an effort to duplicate their earlier success!"

"There's plenty of time and opportunity to hit more of those," said Nick. "During the week try to practise all that I've taught you this lesson so that you will be in perfect shape to tackle our next obstacle – the woods. I'll also introduce you to the rest of the clubs you can carry in your golf bag."

The following evening I was at the golf driving range practising *sensibly*, with an encouraging degree of success. I couldn't wait to come to grips with the woods!

Left: Always execute a full follow through extending your arms high so that the clubhead finishes over your left shoulder.

Lesson 4 - Into the woods

Before starting my next lesson, Nick was as good as his word and introduced me to the clubs you can carry in your bag during a round of golf.

"You can carry a maximum of 14 clubs in your bag – but you are unlikely to need anything like that number for quite some time," said Nick. "The club you have been using to date – the 7 iron – is, in my opinion, one of the easiest clubs to use, and also one of the most versatile, which is another reason why I introduced you to it before all the others.

"The 7 iron is the perfect club with which to 'manufacture' shots, particularly if you have got to know and trust it. It is the club I use, for example, for *chipping* the ball on to the green. You can use any iron for chipping, but I would advise the 7 iron because its length and the angle of its face are ideal for the role. But I'm getting side-tracked. I want to show you, briefly, the complete range of clubs you can use on a golf course, so that you can appreciate why it is so necessary to use a wood without trepidation."

Getting to know the clubs

Nick took all the clubs from a bag and held them in a fan in front of his body. He asked me to notice the difference in length between the clubs, and the different angle of their 'faces'. He then explained that, in his bag, he carried a driver, a 3 wood, a 5 wood, a 4 iron, a 5 iron, a 6 iron, a 7 iron, an 8 iron, a 9 iron, a pitching wedge, a sand iron and a putter.

"Which clubs you choose to carry in your bag," he continued, "will depend on the type of course you're playing and the weather conditions. If, for example, there is a very strong wind blowing, then you might choose a less lofted club to keep the ball low off the tee and for long approach shots."

I then asked why there are so many clubs and Nick replied, "Each club is designed to propel the ball a certain distance, and that distance is determined by the length of the club and the angle of its face. The 7 iron you've been using is classed as a 'middle iron' and is designed for playing shots into the green, with accuracy. The 'certain distance' that a ball can be hit with each of the clubs, is, of course, dependent on just who is swinging the club. Generally speaking, however, the difference between each club is about ten yards."

Looking at the first tee and then at the first green far in the distance, I observed that it did not seem very far.

"When you are on the green," said Nick, "and about to putt, ten yards seems a very long way indeed. Don't be misled by the fact that golf is played on a pitch that covers a vast area. The idea is to get the ball as near as possible to the hole with each shot, without getting into any trouble on the way. The nearer you can get the ball with each successive shot, then the more chance you have of actually getting the ball to disappear *down* the hole – which is, of course, the ultimate aim. Remember that multiplying ten yards by even ten clubs equals 100 yards, and 100 yards is quite some distance."

"You shouldn't hit the ball *harder* the further you have to go, but rely on the club to gain you the necessary distance," explained Nick. "The woods are your 'heavy artillery' – designed to enable you to hit the ball the furthest possible distance, with the least possible effort. If you can drive off the tee and use your woods off the fairway with confidence, then you will not only find golf a tremendously satisfying sport, but also a much easier one. Unfortunately, most golfers find their woods the most difficult clubs to use. This is because the wood has an appreciably longer shaft than your 7 iron, for example. You,

When using a wood you should alter your set-up slightly in order to accommodate a longer club. Adjust the ball position and widen your stance. *Inset:* The follow through of a wood swing.

therefore, have to stand further from the ball when you address it, and so it *seems* a more difficult target to hit.

"In fact, it is not really more difficult," said Nick, "providing you follow the rules I've taught you. Most people, however, get a wood in their hands, see the lovely big head on it, and forget everything they've been taught about the grip, the set-up, rhythm, tempo and timing. They try to *hit* the ball – with little success. One thing to remember when you are using a wood is that any mistake you make will appear to be much greater than it would with your 7 iron.

"The reason is that the wood is designed to hit the ball a long way – so any mistake you make will inevitably be magnified. A slight slice with a 7 iron might see you on the edge of the green, rather than nestling in the shadow of the flag. A similar degree of slice with a driver could very well result in you spending a frustrating time deep in the undergrowth searching for your ball. Having said that, however, there are no special errors associated with wooden clubs, only the usual ones magnified."

Adjusting to a wood

"When using a wood, your grip should stay exactly the same," he said, "but because the wood is a much longer club than the 7 iron, you will have to stand further from the ball. Clubs vary in length from about 3ft to 3ft 6in, which may not seem a lot, but can make an appreciable difference – as I think you'll find. With a wood, you have to use a wider swing. Try the exercise I showed you to find out how far you should stand from the golf ball."

I took the wood that Nick offered me, laid its front leading edge square to the target behind the ball, and let the grip fall towards me. Rather than resting just above my left knee, the butt end of the club came half way up my thigh. I shuffled backwards until the club was resting a couple of inches above my left knee, and Nick told me that I was about the right distance from the ball for using a wood. I seemed to be peering at a small yellow dot rather than a golf ball. I felt as if I were miles away from the ball.

"Once I've got you in the correct address position, you'll find that you can hit the ball just as effectively with your wood as you can with your 7 iron," was Nick's response. "I'd also like you to widen your stance – which should be at its maximum width when you are using a wood. You should feel balanced and on a firm base – which you'll need to be because you will be swinging your club in a wider arc. It's important that you feel comfortable, but if you widen your stance too much, you'll find it difficult to achieve a full turn of your hips and shoulders."

I adjusted the width of my feet and Nick nodded his head approvingly. "When you were using the 7 iron, the ball was in the middle of your stance. I now want it lined up with the inside of your left heel, and this is critical when you are using a wood. You'll remember last lesson," said Nick, "I explained to you why, when using an iron, it is desirable to take a divot after your club hits the ball. The club hits *down* to get the ball in the air. The ball is, therefore, positioned in the middle of your stance. When you are using a wood, however, you should aim to make contact with the ball just as the head of your club is beginning to make its *upward* sweep."

"Surely, if the club is beginning to rise at the point of contact it will cause me to top the ball?" I asked. "That is why the positioning of the ball when using a wood is so critical," said Nick. "If your club makes contact with the ball too late, you will, indeed, top the ball and send it skip-

Left: Shout 'fore' or 'take cover' if your ball is flying towards another player.

Right: **Wood swing**
1. The full backswing with the wood.
2. After impact make sure you keep the club on line to the target.
3. Finish high, making sure you turn your body as you hit through the ball. Your weight should now be on your left side.

hopping down the fairway – or into the rough. If your club makes contact too early, you will hit the ground before the ball, fluff the shot completely, and give yourself aching wrists into the bargain."

I asked about using a tee peg with a wood. "When you are on the teeing ground, you use a tee peg," replied Nick. "You're not, however, allowed to use it again once you've played your first shot. It is possible to hit a wood from the fairway without the aid of a tee peg – although many beginners find this a very difficult shot to play." I felt I would be more confident of making good contact with a wood if I could tee the ball up.

I asked Nick if there was any difference in the swing or set-up when playing a wood off the tee or from the fairway. "Not really," he replied. "Playing off the tee is, obviously, the easier of the two shots – but not necessarily, if you are using a driver. This is because a driver has a very straight face. Most of the clubs in your bag have lofted faces designed to help you get the ball up in the air. The driver is designed for distance. The ball will rise, but more in the upward curve of an aircraft taking off, and then only if you make perfect contact. It is not an easy club to use, even from the tee, and so, for the time being, we will concentrate on using a 3 wood – as this club has a more lofted face."

I was sure that I could hit the ball a mile with such a weapon as a driver and said as much to Nick. "You might well be able to use a driver," Nick replied, "but first I want you to gain confidence by using a 3 wood from the tee. You really will have more chance hitting a solid shot with the 3 wood than the driver. Many professionals seldom take the driver from their bag, because the margin for error is so very small. The whole object of the game of golf is to get round the course in as few shots as possible. When you get out on the course, I want you to think 'score low'. The best way to achieve this ambition is to be sensible – and being sensible means not taking any foolhardy risks, and using a club you feel confident and at home with.

"It's no good hitting the ball over 200 yards if it's 200 yards into deep rough. A far better shot is

1
2
3

Left: The loneliness of the golf hacker.

a 3 wood hit 170 yards right down the middle of the fairway. Spending most of a round of golf up to your neck in the rough stuff and into the woods isn't very enjoyable. I know, because I've had days when, through being foolhardy and using my driver from the tee, just about every tee shot has ended in trouble. If I had been sensible, I'd have realised that my driver just wasn't going to 'behave' itself and opted for a few less yards per drive – and a few less shots per hole."

Hitting from the tee and the fairway

"But you say that hitting a wood from the fairway is even more difficult than teeing off?" I asked. Nick replied, "Most golfers, and particularly beginners, do find it more difficult to 'clip' a ball from the fairway – for obvious reasons. The ball has to be swept away very cleanly, so you have to take great care that the ball is just in line with the inside of your left heel when you address it. You don't want to take a divot when using a wood off the fairway. What you want to achieve is clean contact – with the front leading edge of the club just skidding the turf before it meets the ball. After the ball has been sent sailing away towards your target, you should be able to see a scuff mark on the turf where the ball was lying, not the deep trench left by a divot. The wood is designed with a broad base to make it possible to skid along the turf, without digging in – if used correctly!

"If the ball is on a tee, you have more chance of getting the ball to rise when using a wood. A bad shot will not, however, miraculously become a good shot just because the ball is sitting up invitingly! So, don't be intimidated by hitting a wood from the fairway, because if you can use a wood effectively from the tee, then there is no reason why you shouldn't do the same from the fairway

Below: When teeing the ball up and using a wood, tee the ball so that at least half the ball is above the clubface. Do not tee the ball too high or too low.

– providing you don't try and *scoop* the ball up off the turf. If you do this, you'll sway back and your swing will come through too early, and as a result, you'll top the ball and probably leave an unwanted smile on its surface."

I asked Nick what he meant by 'smile on its surface' and he explained, "The surface of a golf ball is all too easy to cut. The manufacturers have succeeded in making more durable golf balls, but a full-blooded swipe with a wood against the face of just about any ball will damage its surface. Too many topped shots with a wood can be expensive, not only in terms of the shots you'll drop, but also in the number of balls you'll have to buy. If you 'put a merry grin' on to a golf ball, don't carry on using it because a cut in the surface of a golf ball can dramatically change its flight. Think how frustrating it would be to hit a perfect shot, only to find your ball hooking away into the scrub because of a cut in its surface. Golf is a difficult enough game without you handicapping yourself with faulty or damaged equipment."

Getting the teeing height right

"Another vitally important point, and one often ignored," said Nick, "is how high you tee the ball. You should tee the ball so that about half of it is showing above the top of the face of your wood. Don't be tempted to tee the ball up too high. It can *look* very inviting perched in the air begging to be hit, but a ball that is teed too high can become an elusive target.

"This is because it's all too easy for your club to skid *under* the ball. The usual result of such 'contact' is that the ball flies high into the atmosphere and comes back to earth about 50 yards from you with re-entry burns on its sides. It's very frustrating to swing perfectly and have everything correct, only to find that a ball which should have travelled at least 150 yards straight down the middle has travelled about 100 yards into the sky, and only 50 yards down the fairway! So, don't tee the ball up too high."

"What about teeing it up (or down) too low?" I asked. "If you tee the ball too low," said Nick, "you lose the benefit of the tee, and make your drive as difficult to play as a wood played off the fairway. There is, however, nothing wrong in teeing the ball low, providing you always do so, and feel confident that you can hit the ball cleanly off the tee. Most people, however, tee the ball too low by accident, and top their tee shot."

I placed a ball on the tee, and made sure that about half of it showed above the face of the 3 wood. "By all means, have a go," said Nick, "but first make sure that you're gripping the club correctly, that your set-up is correct, that you are aligned square to your target, that you have created enough distance between yourself and the ball to swing effectively, and that the ball is teed up in line with the inside of your left heel."

I was about to launch myself at the ball when Nick warned, "You will, of necessity, have to use a wider swing, so concentrate on *sweeping* the ball away. Swing slowly and smoothly, keep your head down, your eyes on the ball, and, above all else, don't try and hit the ball too hard!"

I concentrated, swung gently, and the ball flew away straight down the middle. I was delighted – but as the lesson continued I found it increasingly difficult to recapture the glory of my first shot with a wood. "You're beginning to think about it a little too much," said Nick, "and as a result you are not swinging smoothly. Let the club head swing smoothly through the arc, sweep the ball away, and then finish high and extend towards the target. Whatever you do, don't get disillusioned. You're doing very well. Once you've got used to the increased weight and length of the woods, and the fact that you have to

swing wider, you'll soon hit the ball with more consistency."

Consistency was definitely what was required. One shot went down the middle, the next hip-hopped along the turf, the next sliced away dramatically to the right, the next had a vicious hook to the left. The final ignominy came when I left the ball sitting on the tee!

Tips for using the woods

Nick conveniently suggested a break while he showed me some useful tips for using the woods. He placed a ball on a tee, and then stuck two further tees in the ground – one about 12 inches in front of the ball, and the other about 12 inches behind it, saying that this was the line he wanted my club to take. He then demonstrated. The ball flew down the very middle of the practice ground, and all three tee pegs were scattered.

Nick then said, "You have a go now, but without the ball on the tee. It's a good idea to get used to 'clipping' the tee the ball rests on when driving, so try and clip all three as you swing *through* the imaginary ball to the target."

"Why is it a good idea to clip the tee," I asked. "I thought that the idea was to hit the ball *off* the tee." "If you don't clip the tee," said Nick, "and try and hit the ball cleanly off it, then you'll be in danger of topping the ball. It's always safer to 'take a little of the tee' when you drive. Try clipping those three tees."

I was not very successful. The front tee refused to move as my club swooshed past it. "That's because you're swinging inside on your follow through," said Nick. "Try and get that

Right: Practising the correct set-up procedure for the woods and finding out how far to place yourself from the ball.

extension *towards* the target. I don't want to see you 'swinging round the corner'. Your swing is going to be wider when using a wood, but it shouldn't become too flat. Try again and hit *through* that imaginary ball on the central tee and then extend towards your target. You should finish in a nice high position."

I swung, and all three tees leapt dutifully from the ground. I swung a few more times with the same satisfying result. Finally, Nick seemed confident that I was swinging on line, and placed a ball on the middle tee. "There's your ball, and there's your target. Align yourself and swing smoothly. Remember to *sweep* that ball away. I'll leave your two guiding tees in the ground for the moment."

I went slowly through my set-up procedure and tried to swing as smoothly as possible, with very gratifying results. The club met the ball with a nice clunk and flew straight down the middle. "There, see what you can do when you concentrate," said Nick. "That was a perfect golf shot. Try again, and remember to set yourself up with care." I did, and achieved the same success – again and again. But now Nick insisted on taking the tee pegs away. I protested – they made an incredible difference and I wanted to use them when playing the course.

This was impossible, as Nick explained. "They are, quite rightly, classed as a technical aid. Just imagine that they are there, or do what a number of great golfers do, which is to pick out a point directly in line to your target about 18 to 24 inches in front of your ball. Look at that point and imagine that you are going to hit the ball

Left: The correct address position for a wood. The stance is wider and the ball is lined up with the inside of the left heel.

right over it. Don't look at that point as you swing, however, but just before it. You've got to focus all your attention on the ball when you are actually swinging!"

"Should I look at any part of the ball?" I asked. "I find it helpful to look at the back of the ball," said Nick, "at the point where I want to ball to make contact with my club. Try it, you might find it helpful." I tried both tips, and the ball sailed away, once more straight down the middle. I was ecstatic – I had done it without anything to aid me. Nick, too, was pleased but said that the lesson had come to an end. As before, I was too excited to stop and wanted to try taking a wood off the fairway.

Nick was insistent, "Let's not spoil what you've achieved today. You've done tremendously well and are hitting your woods with great confidence. I don't want to shatter that confidence at the moment. If you continue to hit your woods well from the tee, then perhaps you can try to hit a wood or two from the fairway when I take you round the course."

"Next week," said Nick, "I want to introduce you to the subtle arts of the short game, which is always a vital part of the game of golf, but even more vital for the beginner. Quite simply, this is because the beginner is unlikely to fire his approach shots on to the putting surface with any regularity. More often than not, the beginner (even one with your undoubted potential!) will find his or her ball near the green, but not actually on the putting surface. So, good chipping, wedge shots, and putting – when you actually get on the green – can save a great many shots."

Importance of mastering the woods

As we made our way back to the club house, I asked Nick whether he believed it absolutely necessary to master the woods if you wanted to be a good golfer. I had observed many professionals going around a course very successfully without reaching for their woods. Nick answered, "For the average golfer, it is essential to be able to use the woods confidently. A few long-hitting professionals do prefer to rely on their 1 or 2 irons from the tee, but usually only on 'tight' courses – those where the fairways are very narrow and accuracy is more important than length."

I queried the use of a 1 or 2 iron rather than a driver. "Presumably," said Nick, "it is because they believe they can hit straighter with a 'driving iron' than a wood, and are prepared to sacrifice a few yards in length for accuracy. These professionals, however, can hit immense distances with their irons.

"The average golf course only has three or four short holes where you can reach the green by taking an iron from the tee. That leaves 14 or 15 holes where a wood of some description really is necessary. If you can play your woods confidently, even if only from the tee, then you'll find that it makes the game of golf far simpler. If you can then learn how to play a wood from the fairway with confidence, you'll soon be looking at the long Par 5 holes as 'birdie opportunities' rather than as frighteningly long challenges. My advice to any golfer is – persevere with your woods – it's well worth the pain and anguish you might have to suffer on the way!"

As we entered the club house, I asked about the irons and why we were going straight from the woods to the short game. "I'm not really missing them out," Nick answered. "You've learnt very effectively how to use a 7 iron, and your grip, set-up and swing for the 3 iron is identical – as you'll find when we get out on the course. I don't intend to devote a separate lesson to the irons and I'll tell you why over a drink."

The wood swing, showing the correct address position, the top of the backswing and the follow through to the finish.

The irons

"A great many golfers seem to get a psychological block when they are using their long irons, in particular," said Nick. "I don't know how many times I've heard someone say: 'I was hitting my 6 iron like a dream today, but my 3 iron play was as dreadful as usual'. It is easy to say and, perhaps, difficult to put into practice, but there is no rational reason why a person who is hitting 6 iron shots like a dream should have trouble with a 3 iron. The grip is the same, the set-up the same, and the swing the same. The difficulty must lie in the mind. It is true that the 3 iron has a slightly longer shaft than the 6 iron and a relatively upright face, but these differences should not have any detrimental effect on the ability to use the club.'

"But surely the flat face and the longer length make the 3 iron more difficult to use?" I asked.

Nick disagreed. "If you grip the club correctly and set yourself up methodically, then you should have no difficulty with longer irons. When you look at a 3 iron and its relatively upright face you may think you have to *help* the ball into the air. If you do this, you will probably scoop the ball and end up topping it. If you can remember to hit down on to the ball whenever you are using an iron club, then the ball will go up." Nick went on, "You use exactly the same swing for a 3 iron as for the 7 iron but you widen your stance a little when using the longer irons. This is to compensate for the slightly longer length of club you will be swinging."

Choosing the correct iron

Nick explained why there were so many irons to choose from. "The whole idea is to get the ball from tee to green and into the hole in the least

Enjoying a refreshing soft drink with Nick in the clubhouse at Redbourn.

number of shots. How you achieve it, and what clubs you use, are a matter of personal preference. There is nothing clever in hitting the ball harder than you need to. The reason why there are so many irons to choose from is because each one gives you extra length. If you underclub and use a pitching wedge when you should be using an 8 iron, then the chances are that you will hit too hard – with disastrous results. If you can learn to play within yourself, then you will be a more controlled and successful golfer. You will also have more fun!"

"Because the important thing is to try and hit within yourself, it is good advice to take a longer iron club than you think you need. I've found that women are much more sensible when it comes to club selection. I've taught some men who, even though they were (and are) pretty good golfers, had no idea when it came to choosing which club to use."

Judging distance

Nick pointed out that I would soon learn how far I could hit the ball with each iron club. "Once you are hitting the ball confidently with your irons, you can then go down to a driving range and hit five or ten shots with each one. Most driving ranges have distance markers. If you make a note of how far you hit each ball with each club, you'll then be able to take the average. Ignore, of course, any shots that you fluff or top! Having done that, most golfers need to know how far from the hole they are when on the course, and this can be difficult. Some golf courses have distance markers, but most, unfortunately, do not – so judging distance is something you'll have to learn through experience, or by purchasing one of the pocket distance range finders on the market."

Nick, however, advised common sense. "Remember that on each tee and on your scorecard, it will tell you exactly how far you have got to go from the teeing ground to the hole. After you have hit a drive, pace it out. This should give a good idea of how far you've got to go to the flag. Once you've done this 'pacing' a few times, you will quickly become a better judge of distance. Remember, however, the golden rule – don't underclub and hit too hard. A gentle swing with a 4 iron is likely to be far more effective than a hard swipe with a 6 iron – if that is the choice of clubs you have in your bag. Quite obviously, if you have a 5 iron, that is the club you should use!"

"What you need to know about iron play is best learned on the course," continued Nick. "When we start playing a round, you'll soon discover that the ball seldom lands exactly where you would wish it. Even a ball hit straight down the fairway from the tee can be the victim of an indifferent lie which can affect the choice of club, or the type of shot that needs to be played. You won't be changing the essential elements of your swing, but you will have to change certain elements of your set-up to meet the challenge of uneven lies, thick rough, a howling wind, or any number of other natural elements that make golf so very challenging!"

Lesson 5 - The short game

I was looking forward to my next lesson, which was to be learning the short game. I was sure that putting was definitely my strong point, as I sometimes beat my former husband when we played carpet golf to while away the time in hotel rooms around the world. Predictably, I was soon to discover that there is a world of difference between hotel carpets and golf course greens.

When I arrived for my next lesson Nick took me not to the practice ground but to an area in front of a practice green, uncomfortably near the windows of the clubhouse restaurant. Ignoring any onlookers, he began, "Golf's short game should be practised as much, if not more, than any other golfing art. In fact, Gary Player has said that a golfer should spend at least four times as much on the short game as on the long game, if he or she wants to perfect golf. A great many beginners are so relieved when they get to within 50 or 60 yards of the green that they forget that the whole purpose of the game is to get the ball down the hole, in *as few shots as possible.* On numerous occasions I've seen beginners astound themselves by hitting a good drive straight down the middle, then another good iron to within spitting distance of the green, only to ruin everything by taking a wedge and fluffing the ball – they then attempt to chip and hit the ball through the green and down a bank on the other side. In short, what should have been a par hole, becomes a bogey, a double bogey, or even a treble bogey!"

"As you are probably aware," Nick continued, "a treble bogey is three shots over the 'par' for the hole. Each hole on the golf course is either a par 3, a par 4, or a par 5 – depending on its length. On a par 3 – a short hole – for example, to score a treble bogey you would have to score a 6, a double bogey would be a 5, and a bogey a 4. A 'birdie' is 'one under par' and on a par 3 hole, a birdie score would be 2, and an 'eagle' would be a hole in one – and the acclaimed albatross is very rare in golf. This is three shots under par – and only usually achieved on a par 5 hole when the lucky golfer manages to hole his second shot, which will undoubtedly be a shot of all of 200 yards!"

'We're getting side-tracked again," said Nick. "Let's get back to the intricacies of the short game. It's always worth reminding yourself that a shot dropped around or on the green counts exactly the same as a shot dropped when you top a drive. A good short game can rescue your score, even if you have reached the green 'along the ground' after a succession of topped shots. If you can then pitch or chip on to the green to within a few feet, and then hole your putt, you can still end up with a fairly respectable score."

"A pitch shot," Nick explained, "is one where you use one of your most lofted club – your pitching wedge if you have one – and send the ball high through the air right to the green. I would advise that you only use a pitch if you have an obstacle such as a bunker, a ditch, or a high bank to carry. And this is because a pitch shot is far more difficult for a beginner to control than a chip shot. With a chip shot, the idea is to keep the ball as close to the ground as possible. You only make it airborne to cover a patch of short rough or the fringe of grass in front of a green. The aim is to let the ball run as much as possible along the ground. As this is the shot I want you to use, unless you absolutely *have* to pitch, I'll teach you it first."

Left: Chipping out of trouble. Nick advises on how to chip out of the semi-rough and from behind a tree. In the short game, the chip and run shot is a most effective way of getting the ball close to the hole.

Lesson 5

Chipping. In order to chip well, the feet should be quite close together with the ball in the middle of the stance or towards the left heel, with your weight on the left hand side of the body.

The chip shot

Nick handed me a 7 iron. "This is the club I want you to use for chipping. As I said during an earlier lesson, successful chipping is very dependent upon your ability to 'feel' a shot. It's a good idea to use the same club for chipping, to become so familiar with it that you feel confident it will obey your commands."

"Why exactly is a 7 iron a good club for chipping. Surely I would have more control with my pitching wedge?" I asked. Nick disagreed. "Remember that, when chipping, the aim is not to send the ball high into the green, but as near the ground as possible. The pitching wedge has too lofted a face for chipping – unless you are right on the edge of the green and close to the flag. In which case, you will want the ball to land as softly as possible. To achieve this soft landing, you want to chip the ball higher than you would do when playing a conventional 'chip and run' shot. The 7 iron is ideal for most chip shots because the angle of its face is enough for you to lift the ball over the grass fringing the green on to the putting surface – from where the ball should roll to the hole." Since I had been practising chipping in my garden, Nick suggested I try it. I got myself in position, swung, and the ball shot from my club and disappeared into the undergrowth on the far side of the green. Clearly there was a different technique for the chip shot which I was yet to learn. There was – and Nick proceeded to demonstrate.

"With the chip shot I want you to open your stance a little, and have your feet very close together," said Nick. I watched as Nick turned his body *towards* the target. "But you're not square to the target," I protested. "I thought you said that I should always keep my body square to the target?" "Not when you're chipping, pitching or playing from a bunker," replied Nick. "I want you to open your stance, and by that I mean slant your feet towards the target. They should also be approximately half as wide apart as normal and your knees should be well flexed, and also slanting towards your target."

Obviously, the rules changed for the chip shot and Nick explained why. "This is because the left side of your body should dominate the chip shot. I want you to swing the club smoothly, but I don't want you to get too much 'hip turn' into your swing – and opening your stance should prevent the right side of your body from messing things about too much. You should set yourself up with at least two-thirds of your weight on your left side. I don't want you to lean into the ball, just to keep the greater part of your weight on your left foot."

Nick showed me how he wanted me to stand. After lining up square to the target as a routine for every other shot I had learnt, it was disconcerting to be pointing in the wrong direction. I would soon get used to it, Nick assured me, and achieve far greater control – which he stressed was the aim of the open stance. "I don't want you to transfer your weight when you are chipping. Power isn't necessary at all – but accuracy is. The less 'moving parts' you use in a shot, then the more chance you have of being accurate. That's not to say that I want you to be rigid when you address the ball – far from it – but rather that I want you to keep your weight firmly in control, and on your left side."

"Where should the ball be?" I asked. "In the middle of your stance," said Nick. "I also want you to grip down your club. If the grass is particularly thick you should hold the club at least half way down your grip. This will help you achieve greater feel and control. Try it."

I did, and then asked Nick if I could try another chip. He allowed me to do so – but only

after first checking that my set-up was correct and warning me to take my time and swing smoothly. "This little shot is just as important as a drive. Remember it counts the same." I took my time, and swung. The club seemed to travel under the ball, and the ball merely jumped a few inches forward. I looked at Nick in despair. "You 'quit' on your shot," said Nick. "Just because you only have 20 yards or so to go to the flag doesn't mean that the ball is going to get there under its own steam! You've got to swing your club *through the ball*."

I tried again, with the same unsatisfactory result. "You're trying to flick the ball away," said Nick. "In the chip shot, you don't want your wrists to enter into the action. Try to develop a good solid stroke, and keep your hands ahead of the ball at impact. You don't need to lift the ball – your club face will do that for you. Just concentrate on swinging smoothly towards the flag, and try to keep your left arm firm. The impetus for the shot should come from your shoulder action. If you're afraid of hitting the ball too hard, keep your backswing short and follow through smoothly towards your target." "So the softer I want to hit the ball, then the shorter the backswing I should take?" I asked. "Exactly," said Nick. "Shorten your backswing – but keep your rhythm and a nice even tempo – remember not to look up too quickly."

I tried again and made solid contact. The ball, however, went nowhere near to the flag, but scuttled off the left hand side of the green. "Don't worry about where your ball has ended up for the time being," said Nick. "That was much better. Your stroke was much more solid and positive and you kept your weight nicely on your left foot. If you put too much weight on your right side, then your left side will become too sloppy for an effective chip shot and you'll be in danger of trying to scoop the ball towards the hole – which must be avoided at all costs. Try again, but this time attempt to pick an area where you want the ball to land."

I was not sure what Nick meant. "Well," he said, "rather than trying to chip to the flag, try chipping the ball and making it land in an imaginary circle on the way to the flag. Just where your landing circle is will depend on how far you are from the hole, what the lie of the land is like between you and the flag, and how hard the green itself is. It's always a good idea to walk up to any green you are intending to chip on and test its hardness. If the green is rock hard, then your

landing circle will be much nearer to you than it would be on a wet green – where you could afford to chip the ball into a circle much nearer to the flag."

I tried to envisage a circle to land my ball in and swung smoothly. The ball flew through the air, landed in 'my circle' – and ran off the back of the green. "I think your circle was a little too near the flag," said Nick. "This green is relatively hard, so you'll have to aim to land the ball much nearer to you – but your line was good." This was encouraging, since chipping was rather more difficult than I'd imagined. I tried to define an imaginary circle just on the fringe of the green and chipped once more. The ball landed in my circle and ran obediently up to within a few inches of the hole. "Brilliant!" said Nick. "See how easy it is if you stroke the ball rather than scoop it, and keep your left hand moving towards your target."

"That time I just imagined that I was throwing the ball underarm to make it land in a circle and then run up to the flag," I said, flushed with success. "Miraculously, it seemed to work." "That's not a bad way to imagine a chip shot at all," said Nick. "The only thing you have to beware of is trying to scoop the ball in an attempt to put it exactly where you would do if you were throwing it underarm. Mentally rehearse what you want to do by all means, but once you address the ball, don't forget that it is your club that will propel the ball towards the hole! So, remember to take a short backswing, stroke the ball and then follow through towards the flag."

I tried again, and gained Nick's applause by

Left: Perfecting your short game takes hours of practice and requires the development of skills such as 'touch' and 'feel'.

getting the ball to within six feet of the flag. "That's excellent," said Nick. "If you can leave yourself a putt of that sort of length every time you chip, then you will save yourself a lot of shots. But don't worry about that element of the game for the time being. Even if you can't consistently sink putts of that length, you should, at least be able to get down in two shots from six feet – and your aim at the moment should be to try and do just that now your ball is on the green."

"In fact, very few people can consistently hole putts of about six feet in length," continued Nick. "What you should try and achieve when you are chipping is the *opportunity* to have a realistic chance of holing your putt. It's far easier than you might think to take three putts on a green. Unless you can get your chip shots close, then you will be constantly in danger of 'three putting'. Concentrate on getting your chips as close as possible to the flag. Even if you miss the putt you should only be left with a 'tiddler' – and sink that without any trouble. Try a few more chip shots, and remember that any chip that results in only a five- or six-foot putt is really very good."

The succession of chip shots that followed were a mixed bag although I was happy when any chip shot of mine reached and then stayed on the green. Most of my poorer efforts were due, according to Nick, to my habit of wanting to jab the ball rather than stroke it. Others were due to my inability to 'feel' how long a backswing I should take, and one or two were a direct result of the most common of all golfing errors – not watching the ball. Nick was, however, reassuringly optimistic, "Don't worry too much about your ability to get the ball close just yet. Your chipping stroke is technically correct, and you'll find that the necessary feel when chipping will come with time – and practice. I can't stress just how important it is to practise your chipping. I've now taught you how you should do it, so it's up to you to gain confidence through practice."

Chipping

The chip shot differs from the pitch in that it is a low running shot as opposed to a high flying shot. You can select almost any iron to play this shot, but a 7 iron is usually favoured.

1. Your feet should be open only slightly, with the emphasis of your weight on the left side of your body.
2. Make sure that your hands are in front of the ball.
3. Take the club back, breaking your wrists slightly. The shot should feel rather like a long putt.
4. Your head and body should remain still as you swing through with your arms.
5. A good tip: Always look carefully at the slope of the ground before chipping. If you are faced with a downhill chip select a more lofted club , and if you have to chip uphill choose a 5 or 6 iron.

Putting vs chipping off the green

"Wouldn't it have been just as easy for me to have putted some of those chip shots?" I asked. "I'd prefer to see you chipping the ball when you are not actually on the green," replied Nick. "It may *appear* easier – and that is often the problem when taking a putter from off the green – it's tempting and can, therefore, be very dangerous. Most greens are surrounded by slightly longer and fluffier grass – which is called the fringe. Now, knowing just how hard to putt a ball through this grass is really very difficult to judge. If you putt the ball too softly, you'll get stuck in the fringe and be no better off than you were before you attempted your putt. If you strike the ball too hard, then it will pop through the grass and seemingly accelerate across the green and off the other side – again leaving you no better off, and perhaps much worse off."

"Only use a putter when the grass just off the green really *is* short. Such conditions will only normally occur if the golf course itself is naturally hard, or after or during a hot dry summer. Then, and only then, would I advise you to putt. Chipping, once you get to know and trust your 7 iron, really poses fewer problems. You can bypass the troublesome and difficult fringe of grass in front of any green by taking the low trajectory aerial route offered by the chip. It's much safer."

Having heard of a club called a 'chipmaster' specifically designed for chipping, why not use that, I asked, instead of the 7 iron? Although Nick had never used it himself, he said, "It's designed rather along the lines of a putter, except it has an angled face to make the ball rise. It would probably be all right for short chips, but I doubt if you could achieve the necessary control for longer chip and run shots. Try it by all means. You might find it's wonderful. My hunch, for what it's worth, is that you will be better served by your 7 iron, which really is an all-purpose instrument."

Nick went on to explain when one should use a chip shot. "You would normally use a chip shot from anything up to 30 yards from the green. This distance is, however, very dependent upon the hole you are playing and the condition of the course. On some golf holes, the fairway is an open thoroughfare that leads to the green. If you're playing such a hole, and there are no obstacles or hazards between your ball and the flag, then you might even consider using a chip and run shot from up to 60 or 70 yards – particularly if you are not confident of using your pitching wedge and firing the ball 'in high' to the green. I'd prefer you to think of the chip shot as the one to play around the green, and from distances shorter than 30 yards."

The pitch shot

"When there is an obstacle such as a bunker or a high bank between you and the flag," said Nick, "you will have to play the pitch shot." He took up position in front of a cavernous bunker which protected the practice green. "From here, it's obvious that a chip shot wouldn't be suitable. Your attempted chip would only result in your next shot being played from out of that sandy grave! You have got to get the ball up quickly and then, hopefully, to land softly on the putting surface. The way this is achieved is by adroit use of your pitching wedge which has a very lofted face to make your ball rise quickly. You won't have to learn an entirely new technique to use a pitching wedge effectively but you do need to employ a mixture of the stance employed for the chip shot, and use the 'middle section' of the swing you use for longer iron shots. It's not too difficult to learn the technique, but one problem for the beginner is to confidently 'feel' just how hard you should hit the ball."

I watched as Nick demonstrated, making the pitch shot look ridiculously easy. A succession of balls popped up in a lazy arc over the bunker, landed softly on the green, and then ran up to the hole. "I spend a great deal of time practising this type of shot," he said, as if offering an apology for his prowess. "Pitching and chipping really are arts where practice makes perfect. I may be well practised – but far from perfect when compared to some tournament professional golfers who can, literally, pitch a ball over a bunker and make it land on a small disc! They achieve such expertise only through practice."

"When playing a pitch shot," Nick continued,

"your grip remains the same – although it is advisable, as with the chip shot, to hold the club about half way down the grip to improve your control and accuracy. Your stance should be open, with your feet slanted to the left of the target, and your knees flexed." I recognized that the set-up position was identical to the chip shot, and Nick agreed. "You want most of your weight on your left hand side, and your feet relatively close together. I want you, however, to lay the blade of your club open a little – so that the natural loft of the club is increased. The length of our backswing will depend on how far you are aiming to hit the ball. It is unlikely to be any more than a three-quarter swing. From here, I would advise you to use just a half swing. When you swing, you will descend more steeply than for the chip, and hit down cleanly through the ball to get it to rise. Don't try and scoop the ball over the obstacle – which is the mistake most beginners make with the result that their ball normally falls straight into the hazard they've been trying to scoop over! Remember to hit through the ball and take a full follow through, extending your arms towards the target. Try it."

I did, and the ball fluffed gently into the waiting embrace of the bunker. "You 'quit' on that shot and didn't follow through," explained Nick. "I know it's difficult to trust your implement and your technique until you've hit a few effective pitch shots, but that is what you've got to do. Swing through the ball and rely on the open face of your already lofted club and your shortened backswing to ensure that you don't vastly over-hit your target. Try again."

Once again I carefully went through the set-up procedure and swung. The ball flew into the air, cleared the bunker, and just about cleared the green! It landed on the far edge, bounced into some scrub, and buried itself from sight. "A little bit too much ooomph in that one!" said Nick. "Try another, but make sure that you don't swing back too far. The shot you just played was nearer to a full-blooded swing. Just a little half swing, with a good tempo and rhythm." Finally, after six attempts, I managed to clear the bunker and stay on the green.

But Nick was encouraging. "The shot you've just been trying to play was by no means easy. Persevere with your pitching and you'll find that it comes right – with practice. Once we are out on the course, you'll discover that there are different types of pitch shots and chips you'll be called upon to play. You'll soon learn that each and every shot has to be played on its merits. However, if you follow the basic guidelines, with time and practice you'll find that you really can save yourself an awful lot of shots – and retrieve some seemingly hopeless situations with the aid of your 7 iron and pitching wedge."

Pitching

The pitch shot lifts the ball high into the air and is usually played from a distance of about 60 yards or less to the green. This shot will enable you to stop the ball quickly on the green.

1. Use either your sand or pitching wedge, since these clubs have the most loft.

2. Grip further down the club than you would if you were playing a longer shot.

3. Adopt an open stance by turning slightly towards the target. This will mean that your swing will be more upright.

4. Open the clubface a little.

5. In order to get a 'feel' for the shot always take a practice swing first.

6. Work your hands, arms and legs together; and turn your body on the backswing and follow through. In order to play the pitch well you should brush the grass with your club.

Playing a pitch shot. Take up an open stance and turn slightly towards the target. Take the club back on the backswing and brush the grass with your club as you hit the ball before the follow through.

I fully intended to practise because it seemed ridiculous to be able to hit the ball nearly 400 yards in two shots, and be near to the green and then take four shots or more getting down the hole from that position. Nick, however, was impatient to show me how to get out of the bunker.

The bunker shot

"The shot you have to play is a close cousin to the pitch shot, but there are one or two important differences," said Nick. "Although it looks difficult, some beginners actually find the bunker shot easier to control than the pitch shot." Nick then threw a ball into the bunker and demonstrated how it should be done. "Use your normal grip," said Nick, "but, once again, hold the club further down the grip. It's important to get a firm footing, so work your feet down into the sand until you have a solid base. This also enables you to feel how soft the sand is. This is important because when you play a bunker shot near to the green you hit *into* the sand. How wet or dry the sand is will obviously affect the length of the backswing you employ."

"As you probably know," Nick went on, "'testing the surface of a hazard' is against the rules of golf, so you can't use your hands. Use your feet and you'll soon be able to judge just how sticky the sand granules are. Jump in here and tell me how wet or dry you consider this sand to be." I did as instructed, shuffled my feet and came to the obvious conclusion: it was very dry. "Right," said Nick, "so from that little test you know that you are not going to have to use a full swing, by any means, to get the ball out of here. Your sand wedge is designed to cut through the sand and blast the ball out. If, however, the sand was very wet and heavy, you would probably have to take a full swing to gain enough momentum to cut through the sand and bring the ball out at the desired velocity."

"So I don't try and hit the ball *off* the sand?" I asked. "Not in this situation," replied Nick. "Here we want the ball to come out of this sand at a high trajectory to clear the lip of the bunker. In fact, the club face shouldn't actually touch the ball. It is the sand which blasts the ball out and up high and soft on to the green. To achieve this, we use the same technique as for the pitch shot – an open stance and a slightly open club face. Swing the club smoothly and aim to hit down into the sand about two inches behind the ball."

I protested. "Surely all I would achieve would be a great shower of sand with the ball going nowhere." "Remember that it is the sand itself which will explode the ball out, and not the club face," said Nick. "If you hit down into the sand about two inches behind the ball, the club will cut through the sand, and the force of the explosion will blast your ball out in a controlled manner." But what was to stop my club just digging ever deeper into the sand if I hit down into it, I asked. "A sand wedge has a broad rounded base

Bunker shots

Playing well out of bunkers requires a lot of practice. However, here are a few simple rules to help you play this shot:

1. Adopt an open stance by turning towards the target.
2. Flex your knees.
3. Concentrate your weight on the left side of your body.
4. Hit into and through the sand when striking the ball, aiming your club into the sand about 1in (25mm) behind the ball. This lifts the ball up and out of the sand.
5. Hit through the shot to a finish, executing a full follow through.
6. Note: The length of the bunker shot can be varied accordingly: a small amount of sand should be taken for a long shot, and a lot of sand for a short shot.

Getting out of a bunker. Remember to hit into and through the sand when striking the ball *(far left and inset)* and hit through the ball to a finish with a full follow through *(left)*.

which is designed to stop the club burying itself," Nick explained, "and the momentum of your *accelerating* swing will ensure that your club cuts through the sand and blasts your ball out."

Nick then demonstrated. He took a three-quarters swing with a full follow through and the ball seemed to float up from the sand and land gently on the green. I was suitably impressed but ignoring my applause, Nick continued, "There's a couple of other important things to remember when playing bunker shots: one, your club is not allowed to touch the surface of the sand at the address; and, two, you must remember to rake the bunker after you have played your shot. You may not be very successful at first but don't be disheartened. Bunker shots, like chip shots and pitches, require a great deal of practice."

The fairway bunker shot

My first attempt at a bunker shot was, relatively speaking, far more successful than my earlier pitch shots. The ball did come out of the bunker and stay on the green – albeit a very long way from the flag. I decided not to play another and instead asked Nick about something that was puzzling me. Golf courses not only have bunkers protecting the greens, but also strategically placed down the fairways to trap drives. How did one play a bunker shot from that type of hazard?

"When you're trapped in a fairway bunker," said Nick, "you obviously want to try to get the ball out and as far as possible down the fairway. The golden rule, however, is to get the ball out. If your ball is lying in a shallow bunker that doesn't have a high lip between you and your target, you can then attempt to play a normal iron shot and try to 'clip' the ball cleanly off the surface of the sand. This is one of the few occasions when using an iron that you don't try and hit down and through the ball. If your ball is 'plugged' – that is, buried in the sand – then you should revert to the greenside bunker shot to make sure that your ball leaves the bunker. In general terms, the further you want to hit a ball from a bunker, then the more you close your stance. I'll demonstrate this when we get you playing a round. In the next lesson, we'll move on to putting or else you'll get to the green in two shots and not know how to propel the ball down the hole!"

Lesson 6 - On the green

"Putting is the one area of the game of golf where a beginner can afford to be individualistic, and have a more than even chance of getting away with it," said Nick as we walked up on to the practice green. "Just as the putter itself comes in every conceivable shape and size, so golfers with a putter in their hands employ a bewildering number of techniques. There are a few golden rules that should be followed, but, in all honesty, these are nothing like as rigid as those for grip and set-up, and the rhythm and tempo of the golf swing. For example, one rule when putting," said Nick, "is that your left wrist should remain firm and lead the stroke, yet some of the greatest putters in the world are noted for using a very 'wristy' action in their putting stroke!"

"So I can develop my own putting style, providing it works for me?" I asked. "Yes," said Nick. "I would, however, like you to try the conventional technique to begin with before experimenting too much. Although the golden rules are not sacrosanct, they do have the merit of being tried and trusted, and they work for a great many players."

"Some golfers have successfully used a technique whereby they stand with their feet together parallel to the line of their putt, and their right hand well down the shaft on a special grip almost by the hosel of their putter. This is not a technique I would advise, however, unless you really do get very nervous when putting – and then only as a last resort. I suffered what is called the 'yips' very badly a couple of years ago when I was playing tournament golf, but even I wasn't desperate enough to try this side-saddle technique!"

I'd heard about, and actually seen, golfers suffering from the dreaded 'yips' – when even the shortest of putts becomes a nightmare. The unfortunate golfer often develops an involuntary twitch in his or her putting stroke. I hoped and prayed it would not afflict me later on. However, for the moment, I was gratified to know that, as long as my putting stroke looked like a golf shot, I didn't have to follow hard and fast rules.

"I don't want you to think for a moment that I consider putting unimportant," warned Nick. "It is as vital as your ability to send the ball sailing away down the middle from the tee with your wood, if not more so. Never forget that a 20-inch putt on the green counts exactly the same as a 200 yard shot from the teeing ground down the fairway. If you can putt well, then you are likely to beat a great many golfers who hit the ball further and straighter than you, but who can't putt to save their lives. There are a few tips I can give you," continued Nick, "and, of course, the best way to improve your putting is, like so many facets of golf, through practice. Practice will never make you perfect when putting (even the greatest of putters have off days) but it will give you a far better chance of holing those two or three foot putts consistently – and that is what you want to achieve."

"Is there such a creature as a born putter, in your opinion?" I asked, secretly hoping that I might be one. "There certainly is," said Nick, "but even born putters have to practise if they want to really capitalize on their natural talent. Women, for some reason, do tend to be better putters than men. They seem to have a natural sensitivity on the greens that men often struggle to find – and sensitivity, the ability to feel just how hard to hit a given putt and to know the right line, is vital if you are going to be a great putter."

Reverse overlap grip

Much heartened by this, I set about learning all I could about putting, particularly the grip to use. "The reverse overlap grip is the grip I use, and a grip you might like to try," said Nick. "Rather than the little finger of the right hand overlapping the index and second fingers of the left hand, all four fingers of the right hand grip the club, and the index finger of the left hand overlaps the fingers of the right. Your thumbs, in this instance only, should run straight down the middle of the shaft, as this helps you keep both your palms square to the putter face."

I tried it but it felt very strange after the interlocking grip I was used to and now comfortable with. However, Nick suggested I try one or two putts with the reverse overlap grip. "Don't grip the club too tightly," he said, "or this will restrict your stroke. Just as you should never quit on any golf shot, so you must never quit on your stroke when putting– no matter how short a putt faces you. Always swing through the ball. If you can get used to the reversed overlap grip, I believe it should help to improve your sensitivity on the greens. Although Jack Nicklaus normally uses the interlocking grip, he reverts to the reverse overlap when putting– and he's not a bad putter at all! He obviously believes, as I do, that it's easier to 'feel' a putt when you have all four fingers of the right hand on the grip."

Art of putting

I decided that what was good enough for Jack Nicklaus was good enough for me. Nick then showed me what he considered to be a good stance for putting, but stressed that the most important thing was to feel comfortable over the ball and to hit the ball squarely, "It sounds an obvious thing to say," said Nick, "but you'd be surprised just how many golfers bemoan their luck on the greens, and yet do not take the trouble to, firstly, line the blade of their putter square to the target, and, secondly, hit the ball squarely. Putting is a difficult art. Judging just

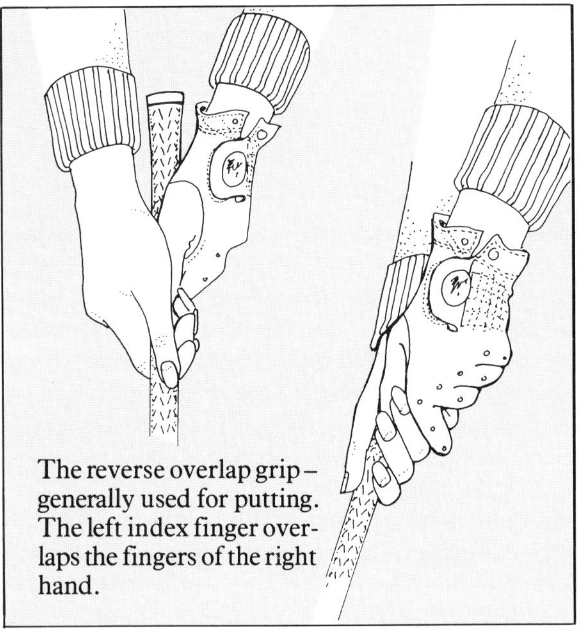

The reverse overlap grip – generally used for putting. The left index finger overlaps the fingers of the right hand.

how hard to hit a putt and 'reading' which way a putt is going to break can, perhaps, only be learnt through experience – unless you are one of the lucky few who seem to know innately where a ball is going to go – so it's essential to aim your putter square to the line you want the ball to travel in. If you don't do that, then there is very little chance you will manage to propel your ball into the waiting $4\frac{1}{2}$ inch hole. There's also a great danger that you will leave yourself with another missable putt – which, above all, is what you must try to avoid. When you are putting from any distance, try and imagine that you are putting into a 3 foot wide hole rather than a tiny $4\frac{1}{2}$ inch hole. It can do wonders for your confidence!"

"But would you advise me to putt with a firm left wrist?" I asked. "I most certainly would," said Nick, "as I believe it helps you keep the blade of your putter square to the target *consistently* – and that is the aim when putting – a consistent stroke. You should never poke or jab at the ball, and I firmly believe that your hands, arms and shoulders should all move as one. Again, remember to let your hands *lead the way to the hole*. They should continue to do so after

Address position for putting. Make sure you are comfortable and that your feet are square and your shoulders parallel to the line of the putt.

the ball has been struck. Also make sure that your head remains still – which it will do naturally if you keep your eyes on the ball and don't jerk at the ball. I like putting with my eyes directly over the ball as this helps me to see more clearly the line I want the ball to travel."

I then proceeded to putt a few balls but, alas, found the golf green less friendly than my living-room carpet. I putted the ball towards the hole only to find it swinging away in a dramatic fashion. I also found it remarkably difficult to judge how hard to hit the ball. Some of my putts charged past the hole, others came to a limp stop several feet from the hole. I was relieved to hear Nick say, "Don't worry too much where your putts are ending for the moment. This practice green is very inconsistent and hasn't got the greatest surface. We use it more for pitching and chipping on to, rather than putting. You've got a nice fluent putting stroke but you're having some difficulty getting the right line and judging the pace of the green. When you approach a putt, take your time. Make sure that your putter is square to the target and that you are well balanced and comfortable. Look at the flag and let instinct tell your arms how hard to stroke the ball. Just as you 'know' how hard to place a cup down on a sideboard, so your 'golfing brain' can be relied upon to tell you how hard you need to stroke your putt – but you must be relaxed enough to let the message get through. Putting requires complete concentration, and you must never let your mind wander, get flustered, or rush things.

"Take a bit more time," said Nick. "Try to see in your mind's eye the route your ball will take on its way to the hole. Pick the point where you think your ball will first start to break to right or left on that route – then aim towards that point rather than the hole. Approach the putt as if it

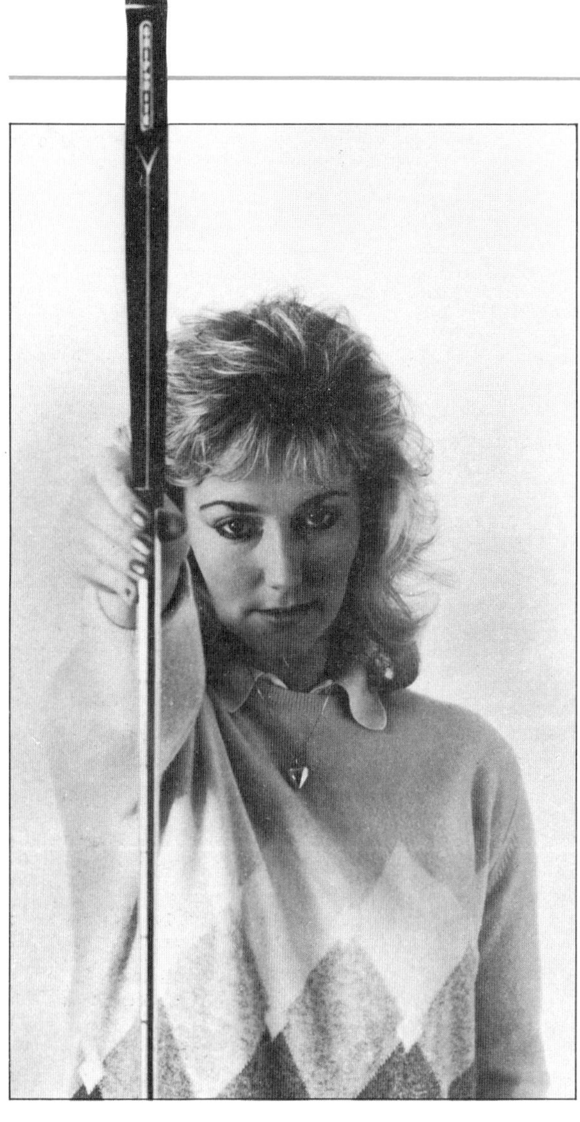

Plumb bobbing is a way of lining up your putt by using the shaft of your club to line up your ball and the hole.

were perfectly straight, stroke the ball smoothly and with a good rhythm." I tried it, and was delighted with the result as the ball snaked its way to the hole before coming to rest about 18 inches away.

Nick had more tips to give me. "Here's a good one if you've got a 'flat putt' – one that you don't expect to break either way. Imagine that there is a straight road from your ball to the hole. Just putt down the white line! Surprisingly enough, it works. Putting is very much a matter of controlling your mind. If you miss a putt, don't get flustered. Just take your time with your next one, and stroke through the ball towards the hole. This is particularly true if you've left yourself a short putt. Try looking at a point in front of the ball over which you want your ball and your putter to pass. That should make sure that your left hand and your putter blade keep moving towards the hole *after* the ball has been struck."

Testing the green

He went on, "A strong wind can affect the putter-head, so you have to beware of that; and a wet green will dramatically take the pace off your putt – so look for wetness before you putt on it. Not all the greens on a golf course will behave in the same manner. Some greens are always drier than others. Just as there are patches of your garden that always seem to be parched, whilst others always seem to be soggy, so there are hard greens and soft greens on a golf course.

"When you play a different golf course remember that it is likely to have greens that behave in a very different way to those you are used to – and that is one of the delights of golf. A bone hard, dry green, such as you find on many seaside or Links courses, is likely to be lightening fast – particularly if the grass has been recently mowed. A ten-foot putt on a dry green might, therefore, require the lightest of strokes, while a putt of equivalent length on a wet green will require a fairly strong putting stroke. The type of grass on the green and the 'nap' of the grass over which you have to putt should also be studied. If you are putting *against* the grain of the green, then you will have to stroke your putt harder than if you were putting *with* the way the grass lies."

"Should the power of the putt be determined by the length of the backswing as is the case with my other shots?" I asked. "There is no hard and fast rule," said Nick, "I prefer to determine the strength of any putt by legthening my backswing; others prefer power to be determined by the length of the follow through, keeping their backswing consistent. At the moment you are favouring the backswing technique and, as you have a nice putting stroke, I wouldn't change it. The golden rule in putting really is to stick with what works for you – and to practise, practise, practise."

Confidence – the clue to putting
Nick looked at his watch – alas, the lesson was over – and we made our way back to the shop. "What's the best advice you've ever been given about putting?" I asked as we entered the shop. "That's easy," said Nick, "don't look to see if the ball has dropped into the hole, but let your ears tell you, and constant practice."

In the shop, I noticed that hickory-shafted putters were on sale. They used to be popular years ago, I knew, but I queried their current vogue. "Some people believe that they can 'feel' their stroke better with a hickory shaft," Nick explained. "I'm not one of them. I prefer to believe that all the technology and money that has been spent on golf club development has achieved something. I'd never dissuade anyone from using a hickory shaft, however, if that is what they believe is right for them. Remember that putting is much more a case of confidence and inspiration than faultless technique. Fortunately for me as a teacher, the same can't be said about the rest of the game of golf – as I think you'll discover next week when I take you round the 18-hole course. I hope you're fit! It's a rather different proposition to the 9-hole short course.

"After next week's round," said Nick, "you might be interested in buying your own set of clubs. The ones I'll lend you for the playing lesson are OK, but you should get acquainted with your own set as soon as possible. You won't have to spend a fortune if you buy a half set, a putter and a bag and, of course, I'll help you find a set that suits you."

I was very impressed at how long it had taken Nick to bring up the subject of club purchase. Retailing is as much a club professional's means of making a living as teaching, and Nick had made absolutely sure that I was right for the game, and the game was right for me, *before* becoming a salesman and trying to sell me any equipment. As he pointed out and talked about various items of golf equipment, I was impressed at both the depth and range of his knowledge. I asked him how he had become a club professional, for how long, and what the job entailed. He was very forthcoming in his answer.

Putting

In preparing to putt, always study the intended line of putt and practise your stroke before addressing the ball.

1. Adopt a comfortable address position, checking that your feet are square and your shoulders are parallel to the chosen line of putt.
2. You may change your grip for putting: the reverse overlap grip where the index finger of the left hand is laid over the fingers of the right hand brings increased control and feel to the stroke.
3. Stand with your feet comfortably apart; and ensure that your weight is balanced evenly on both feet.
4. Position the ball opposite your left heel.
5. Your head should be over the ball and should remain still when you are playing the stroke.
6. Moving your shoulders, hands and arms as one unit, take the putter away from the ball smoothly, keeping your wrists firm.
7. Move the putter-head through the ball, ensuring that it is square as it travels through the ball.
8. The club should accelerate as it strikes the ball, with the clubhead remaining on the intended line of putt.
9. As a general rule, you should always follow through the same distance you have taken the club back.

Profile of a golf professional

"I started playing golf at the age of nine," said Nick, "as I was fortunate enough to live near a pitch and putt course. The pitch and putt course got me hooked on the game, and it wasn't long before I started playing 18-hole courses wherever and whenever possible. The more I played, the lower my handicap fell. By the time I was 16, I was firmly convinced that I wanted to become a professional golfer. All that was necessary was to convince other people that I was good enough! My handicap at the time was 4 – which was considered fairly 'useful' – so I started applying for Assistant Professional posts at golf clubs around my area. I was lucky and got taken on.

"The life of a young assistant club professional certainly isn't glamorous, but it's fascinating – and rewarding – if you love golf. When I started, I was a general dogsbody, doing all sorts of things. On infrequent occasions, I taught. I did, however, have the chance to play in tournaments, and my relative success in these did much to boost both my morale and my prestige at the club. During my first job, I learnt the nuts and bolts of being a club professional – and there is a great deal more to the profession than most people realise."

"Do you have to take any exams before you can become a club professional?" I asked. "Not at the outset," said Nick, "but if you want to become PGA qualified and a teaching professional (which is now my present status), then you first have to prove to the PGA (the Professional Golfer's Association) that you have the playing ability, the necessary all-round knowledge, the teaching ability, and the business acumen."

"How do they find out whether you have the playing ability?" I asked. "Through your handicap?" "You have to pass a playing ability test which is held on the Derby course at the Belfry and shoot two rounds in the lower 70s, which isn't easy!" said Nick. "You then go to Lilleshall, the PGA Training Centre for a week and undergo a pretty intensive series of practical tests and exams, including club repair – most people don't know that club professionals are trained in this craft. It is, however, a very important area of our work. We like to feel that we are not only the teaching experts, but also the equipment experts. If you've just spent upwards of £500 on a set of golf clubs, and damage one of your irons, you'll thank the club professional who can repair it efficiently! We are here to offer a service to the club golfer and to promote the game of golf as effectively as we possibly can.

"I went to Lilleshall in 1983, and since then I have been teaching golf full time, seven days a week. During the summer, it's not uncommon for all of us here to work a 70-hour week – so you can see we earn our money. I spend a great deal of my time teaching people how to play golf and, like anything else, the more you do, the better you get. I can now see faults a lot more rapidly than I used to be able to, and, perhaps more importantly for the individual pupil, I try to find a simple remedy for rectifying faults."

"Have you ever taught anyone who you considered a complete no-hoper?" I asked. "Only one or two," said Nick, "out of a great many. The beauty of golf is that it can be played well by people who don't generally have an aptitude for sport. The natural ball player does tend to pick the game up more quickly than an untrained beginner, but after a short time they can be evenly matched out on the course. Golf is very much a thinking game. The player who 'thinks'

Right: Teaching beginners the art of golf requires patience and an even temperament. Luckily, my coach, Nick, possesses both qualities.

"I think that every club professional in his heart of hearts would like to be out there with the likes of the Langers and the Ballesteros' of this world."

when out on the course, and knows his or her limitations, can make up dramatically for any deficiencies in terms of natural ball playing talent. The handicap system is also a great equaliser. I'll tell you how that works when we play the round next week."

"What about those you couldn't teach?" I asked. "I'm afraid they just didn't have any coordination whatsoever," replied Nick. "The other difficult people to teach are those who can't absorb information. They normally fall into the category of long term players who find it difficult to believe that the grip they've been using for ten years can possibly be wrong!"

"It's obvious that you enjoy teaching," I said, "but what about playing in tournaments?" "It's very difficult to get the right balance between one's duties as a club professional and the lure of the tournament circuit," stated Nick. "I think that every club professional in his heart of hearts would like to be out there with the likes of your former husband, the Langers, and the Ballesteros' of this world. The problem is that to be an effective tournament golfer, you have to *regularly* play tournament golf. Dipping your toe in the water occasionally, as I do, and expecting to do well really isn't on. Perhaps some day soon I'll have sufficient money to make a sustained and realistic attack on the tournament circuit. The European Tour, however, gets more difficult by the year, so for the moment, I'm more than happy teaching the intricacies and delights of the game to people like you."

During the following week, I took Nick's advice and practised constantly – not only my putting, but also the other elements of my game. Fit though I was, I discovered in my next lesson that playing 18 holes of golf is rather more demanding than walking around a golf course as a spectator.

Lesson 7 - Out on the course

Keeping dry on the golf course. An umbrella is an essential part of the golfer's equipment, as is a loose waterproof suit.

The day for my first ever full round of golf turned out bright and breezy. I arrived at Redbourn to find Nick sorting out a set of clubs for me to play with. First of all, he suggested that we should do some warming-up exercises and hit a few balls before stepping on to the first tee. As we headed for the driving range, a summer shower was passing overhead.

'This rain will make the greens slower," observed Nick. "It also has the habit of putting a chill into your bones, so these warming-up exercises are even more vital than ever. Never step on to the first tee without having first warmed up. Where your first drive goes can dramatically affect the whole of your mental approach to the round. Make sure that you are thoroughly warm or else you could find yourself searching for your ball in the long stuff – and that's no place from where to play the second shot of your round – particularly if the only place you are warm is under the collar!"

Warming-up exercises. Place a club under your arms and behind your back. Turn to the right and left to stretch your golfing muscles and move the hips.

Warming up

We entered the covered driving range and Nick started with the first exercise. He placed a club behind his back and hooked one arm over the grip, and the other over the shaft at the other end of the club near the hosel. He then rotated his body until first the head of the club pointed at the ground, and then the grip. He asked me to try it, telling me that it would help to stretch the golfing muscles I would soon be using. I tried it, and after a few minutes got used to the stretching rhythm.

The next exercise was one that women golfers could find difficult – at least at the beginning, since it meant gripping two clubs at the same time. The point of the exercise was to swing both clubs and extend towards an imaginary target. The extra weight of the two clubs again stretched the muscles employed in a golf swing. Nick explained that it was a good exercise to get the blood flowing, and one you can do just as effectively with a weighted club. (To weight a club, wrap some lead wire around the hosel of one of your clubs.) After I had tried this a few times, Nick suggested I swing my 3 wood until I felt thoroughly warmed. He then asked me to hit a few practice balls, and to run through the clubs in my bag so that I would at least have a passing acquaintance with them before using them for real out on the course – which was now invitingly bathed in sunshine. I did not do particularly well on the driving range mats and the mat of fake grass and silently prayed that I would do better on the course.

Lesson 7

Playing a round. Teeing up behind the two marker posts and playing the shot.

To the tee

We approached the first teeing ground – the men's tee. "Let me just hit this drive and then we'll walk forward to the ladies' tee and discuss club selection," said Nick. "I'm sure you know, but when you're on the tee and your partner or opponent is about to play, make sure that you stay well out of his or her vision – and never stand in front of the ball even if you believe that you are standing in a place where the ball can't possibly fly. I like my opponent to stand some distance away from me, behind the ball, but not behind me! The best and most courteous thing to do is to ask your opponent where he or she prefers you to stand when they are about to play."

I nodded in acknowledgement, asked Nick where he would like me to stand – where I was, was the reply – and watched as he prepared to play his shot. He carefully went through the set-up procedure, took time lining himself up, and swung smoothly. The ball sailed away down the middle of the fairway, even though Nick had seemed only to stroke it away without any real effort. It was a beautiful shot. "I must have hit thousands of golf shots," he observed, "and more than a few good ones like that, but it's always the last one that gives me the most pleasure. That's what makes the game particularly satisfying, as you'll soon find out."

The par 4

We walked forward 50 yards or so to the ladies' tee. Nick looked at the plaque alongside the tee. "The first thing to find out is how far it is from the tee to the hole. This is not the easiest of starts – 329 yards, Par 4, Stroke Index 6 – with a 'dog-leg' to the right. You'll need all the length you can get if you are to see the flag when you take your next shot, so let's try your 3 wood, not the driver just yet. The fairway on this hole is rather narrow, and even though length is important, I would prefer to see your ball 140 yards or so down the middle than 200 yards away over in that rough stuff to the right – or the left for that matter! Just concentrate on swinging smoothly – after, that is, you have gone through your set-up procedure slowly and carefully. There is no-one behind us, so keep calm and concentrate."

"Where's the best place to actually tee the ball?" I asked. "As you know," Nick replied, "you're not allowed to tee-off in front of those two markers, and you must place your tee in the rectangle immediately behind them. It's no great advantage to tee your ball close to the markers. In fact, I believe it could be psychologically damaging. I've often watched golfers place their tee as near as possible to the 'front line', get into their stance position all too rapidly, and then take an enormous swoop at the ball – which, not unnaturally, ends up in deep rough. This happens when golfers are too 'length conscious', wanting to eke out the very maximum from their drive. It's far more sensible to try to *position* your drive – how far forward to the legal line you tee your ball doesn't really matter. What does matter is to what side of the teeing area you place your ball."

Nick explained, "You tend to slice your wood shots, so I want you to tee your ball as far to the right – not the left – of the teeing area as possible. This is because I don't want you aiming your drive in a way that shows that you *expect to slice*. Think positively. You are going to hit this drive as straight as a die, and I want you to aim your club slightly down the right hand side of the fairway. See that tree just below that fluffy little cloud? That's where I want you to aim."

I aimed the front leading edge of my club square to the target Nick had selected, and checked my set-up position. "Now, remember

to extend towards the target," Nick warned. "When you have finished your follow through, I want you to hold that position. Remember to take the club back smoothly, and then let your club head accelerate down to the point of impact *naturally*. Get those hands working as your club head meets the ball, and then extend towards the target and hold that position." I nodded, went through my set-up, swung smoothly, and the ball flew down the fairway. Unfortunately, the shot seemed to have a sting in its tail as it started to hook viciously to the left. I seemed to have cured my slice, at least for the time being.

Because I had aimed down the right hand side of the fairway, the ball actually landed on the fairway, before scuttling off it into the rough alongside a small bush on the left hand side. As I had remembered to hold my position at the end of the backswing, Nick was able to show me that I had 'come inside' on my follow through. He diagnosed, "I think you are so afraid of slicing that ball that you tried to get too much wrist into the shot, and your hands 'turned' before your club face actually made contact with the ball. That resulted in the hook. Otherwise, it was a good, clean strike. Better that than a topped dribbler. Much more satisfying, even though it means that we've got a harder search for your ball!"

Left: As a courtesy to other players, do not forget to pick up your tee peg when you have played your shot.

In and out of the rough

Finding my ball was not a great problem but deciding exactly what to do with it was. The ball was nestling in very deep rough. My first impulse was to have a go at playing towards the target. This, I thought, could repair the damage done by my hooked tee shot in the most 'yard effective' way. Nick disagreed, "This won't be an easy shot. Rather than try to hit the ball out of here towards the flag, I want you to play out square. You'll then have a much better chance of playing your next shot from the fairway. The reason is that this rough really is rough. It will take all your strength to even get your ball *out* of that little nest. Play square, and then we'll avenge your tee shot when you take your third shot. For the time being, concentrate on getting your ball out of trouble in the easiest possible way."

He advised a special technique. "Keep your basic swing, but bring your club down at a sharper angle than usual to prevent its blade getting tangled in the grass. You must, however, try and play *through* the ball, and carry your swing through to a high finish. If you don't, your ball will just pop up into the air and finish in a similarly undesirable position. Use your most lofted club, your sand wedge for this shot because, obviously, you want your ball to come up as quickly as possible."

I took my sand wedge, ready to slash my ball from the unwanted embrace of the grass. "Now take your time. Don't rush at it," said Nick. "Play a golf shot, not an uncontrolled swipe. Set yourself up, concentrate, and watch the ball." I calmed down, did as Nick instructed, swung, and the ball mercifully flew out of the rough and landed just on the fairway. Nick applauded, declaring he could not have done better himself. I, meanwhile, was aglow with pleasure and satisfaction. I was beginning to discover that even the undesirable shots can be fun to play.

Using long irons

As we made our way the short distance to where my ball now lay, Nick said, "I'd like you to play a 4 iron from here. I know that you've still got well over 200 yards to go to the flag, and feel perhaps that you should take your wood and try and blast one to the green. But this is where being sensible again comes into play. Unless you hit an absolute beauty, you are highly unlikely to get on the green – even with your 3 wood – so let's 'play a percentage shot' and aim to achieve a good position."

I didn't argue, even though the green looked reachable. I was to learn, however, that distance on a golf course can be very deceptive, and that what appears to be in reach is not. At least, after my hooked tee shot and recovery shot I could now see the flag, and this was encouraging. "Aim

Right: In order to get out of the thick rough you should use a sand wedge. Swing your club at a sharp angle and play through the ball.

Using long irons. *Below:* Nick shows the line of the hole. *Right:* Playing a 4 iron to get close to the green by hitting down and through the ball, taking a divot with me.

directly at the flag from here," said Nick. "There is a bunker on the left and a bunker on the right guarding the green, but I don't think you will hit your ball far enough to be in danger of ending in one of them. Just take a nice easy swing and aim to propel your ball towards the flag. Remember to hit *down* in order to get the ball *up*. Whatever you do, don't try and scoop the ball up into the air. Swing smoothly and easily and the club will do the job for you."

I aimed the front-leading edge of my club square to the target and checked my alignment. "Before you swing," Nick interrupted, "I want to tell you about using long irons. When using a 4 iron as opposed to your 7, there is just one difference in technique. I want to you line yourself up with the ball slightly nearer to your front foot. This is because the longer shaft on your 4 iron means that you will need a wider stance to swing the club comfortably. Line the ball up with the inside of your left heel as you would for wood shots – then move back a couple of inches and you should be in the right position."

I manoeuvred into position. "Now remember, you will still be hitting the ball on the downswing," said Nick. "Go through your set-up procedure again. Aim your club, check your grip, your alignment, flex your legs slightly, and swing smoothly. Hit down and through the ball, and don't be afraid of taking a divot. The ground here is much softer than it is on the well-trodden practice ground teeing area, and that shower of rain has softened up the surface." I swung the 4 iron as smoothly as I could, got the club head accelerating into the ball at the point of impact, followed through towards the target, extended, and held my position. A very satisfying divot flew up in front of me and the ball appeared to sail away directly towards the target. It felt tremendous and I couldn't wait to charge down the

fairway in pursuit of my ball. "That shot has very effectively repaired the damage done by your wayward drive," enthused Nick. "You can see from your follow-through position that you have finished nice and high."

Getting out of a divot hole

Impatient to go after my ball, I was almost out of earshot when Nick said firmly, "You must replace your divot!" Of course, I knew this rule but in my enthusiasm had forgotten about it. "I know it's sometimes difficult to remember," he said, "particularly when you've just hit a particularly good shot, or a particularly bad shot, but it is very important to replace your divot. As you will no doubt experience, there really is nothing more frustrating than to hit a crunching drive right down the middle of the fairway, only to discover that your ball has come to rest in a divot hole. You're not permitted to take your ball out of such an 'annoyance', and so you have to play a

Below: As a point of etiquette, always replace your divot. If your ball lands in another player's divot hole, you are not permitted to remove it.

Setting up for a gentle chip and run shot, using a 7 iron. Thinking of an imaginary circle around the flag helps to place the ball more accurately.

difficult recovery shot rather than a simple pitch into the heart of the green."

Nick also reminded me that he had a ball to play as well, and we walked to where it was lying in the middle of the fairway about 50 yards nearer the flag than mine. As we walked, Nick explained what to do when one's ball *has* landed in a divot mark. "The shot you play depends on how deep the divot is," said Nick, "but the golden rule is not to be too greedy. It's no good ignoring the fact that your ball has ended up in a divot, and trying to play a 4 iron when you might have been much better advised to take a 7 iron. If the ball is deep in a divot, then you'll probably have to use the 'steeper angle of attack' type of shot – which you used to such good effect when blasting out of that deep rough a minute or two ago. If your club makes contact with any obstacle (except sand) before making contact with the ball, then you are likely to end up with a fluffed shot of some description or another."

As we approached his ball, Nick took a 4 iron from his bag, went through his set-up procedure, and then fired a long iron right on to the green. The ball landed in the heart of the green, bounded forward, and then came to a rapid halt. I'd obviously seen my former husband hit countless such shots, and knew that to get the ball to stop so quickly depended on back spin. Nick explained further, "I made very good contact with that ball and, unusually for such a long iron shot, the ball 'bit' as it hit the green and came to a rapid halt. It's only really possible to get a ball to bite in that fashion if the greens are well watered, yielding and receptive. Imparting such backspin is much easier when you are using a more lofted

Nick helping with the chip and run. In this instance, the secret was to let instinct dictate the length of the backswing and to stroke the ball cleanly.

club and attacking the ball from a steeper angle. I did, however, take a calculated risk with that shot. If the ball hadn't bitten, then I would have been playing my next shot from somewhere over the back of the green – and I wouldn't have looked so clever!"

We walked towards my ball which was, as Nick had said, lying short of the bunkers guarding the green about 40 yards from it. I asked Nick if it was always necessary to play a complete recovery shot when in the rough. "Golf is a game of variables," said Nick, "and that is what makes it challenging. With more luck, your ball might have been sitting up on a clump. If that had been the case, you might have tried a long recovery shot. I believe it is often easier to hit the ball cleanly from a 'perched' lie with a wood, rather than a long iron. The iron tends to scythe into the grass; the wood can skim the surface of the grass if you try to sweep the ball away. However, such a shot is risky. If you ever play a course where the rough consists of heather, then the 4 or 5 wood can come in very handy. In heather, which is very tangly stuff, an iron club has to be swung with great velocity if it is to make good contact with the ball. The heavier head of the wood *can* be used to sweep the ball away. Again, I stress this is a risky shot, and should only be attempted if the ball is sitting up."

The chip and run

As we approached my ball, Nick said, "This is a perfect position. You can play any kind of shot from here, as you have managed to neatly cut through those bunkers. There's no hazard between you and the hole so you should, perhaps,

Nick attending the flagstick while I play and vice versa *(inset)*. When putting, players can choose to have the flagstick either attended or removed.

attempt a gentle pitch and run from here. As the green is 'holding', a pitch would be very possible, but I think you'll get nearer with your 7 iron." I took my 7 iron from the bag, finding comfort in its familiarity after the 4 iron. "This is a bit further from the flag than we would usually chip the ball from," said Nick. "You won't, therefore, be aiming to pitch on to the green, but into a circle just about in between those bunkers. As the grass there is nice and short, unless you are unlucky and get a nasty kick, your ball should travel in the direction you intend."

Nick walked up to the area between the two bunkers. "Try and land the ball about here. This is your pitching circle. Don't take too long a backswing, and aim to stroke the ball cleanly and sweetly. Let your reflexes take over. Concentrate on this circle, and instinct will tell you just how long a backswing to take."

Nick then moved out of my 'flight path' and I set myself up. As the shot I was about to play was relatively long for a chip and run, I didn't open my stance too much, or I wouldn't have been able to get the necessary shoulder and hip turn. In my mind's eye, I imagined throwing the ball underarm into the pitching circle and swung. The ball did as ordered! It flew low through the air, landed right in the middle of my imaginary circle, bounced a couple of times, and then ran towards the flag. Unfortunately, it pulled up about 12 feet short, leaving me a putt of decidedly tricky length. "The green is much slower than I imagined," said Nick. "That shower has really taken the pace from this green. Sorry about that. I made your pitching circle too close to you, and not near enough to the flag. That's a shame, because you made perfect contact and judged the pace to perfection." I, however, was delighted and relieved at the outcome of my first planned chip and run – and was already warming to the challenge of my long putt.

Nick's second shot had come to rest about 12 yards from the hole, so it was his turn to putt first. He decided he would have the flag out of the hole, so I took it out and laid it on the green well away from his putting area. Nick putted, and ran his ball up to within a few inches of the hole. He asked me whether I would give it to him. I nodded and he said, "I'm glad about that. I have been known to miss the tiddlers! Now, let's look at the putt you have left yourself. It looks perfectly straight, so just imagine that road leading towards a tunnel. Putt along the white line, and the ball should go in."

I lined my putt up, making sure that the blade of the putter was absolutely square to the target. Remembering that the green was slow, I stroked the ball – but rather too vigorously. The ball ran straight down the white line, leapt the tunnel and hit the back of the cup before bobbing out again and coming to rest a good two feet past the hole. "A little too fierce," said Nick. "The green is slow, but not quite that pedestrian! Now, take your time and make sure you sink the ball. This length of putt is all too easy to miss. Remember not to try and tap it into the hole, but *stroke* it. Keep your left hand moving towards the hole *after* you have hit your putt."

I tried to concentrate, took my time – and Nick's advice – and managed to sink the putt. I had scored a six which, Nick remarked, was a very good start. I nodded my head in agreement as we walked to the second tee. A six didn't sound too bad at all – even if it was a double bogey!

The stroke index

On the way to the second tee, Nick explained the stroke index, which he had mentioned at the

Marking the scorecard: check your opponent's score after each hole before you record it. At the end of the round, you sign the card and hand it to the player.

In deference to other players, you should always repair your pitch mark on the green, using a tee peg or a pitch fork.

beginning of the game. "The stroke index refers to the relative difficulty of the hole you are about to play. The second hole, which is a par 3, is considered to be one of the easiest holes on the course, because it has a stroke index of 16. There are only two holes that are considered easier."

"But why have a stroke index?" I asked. "Well, the stroke index," said Nick, "obviously doesn't enter into the professional game as none of the players have a handicap – playing as they all do off 'scratch'. Most golfers, however, have a handicap which is related to their golfing ability. The maximum handicap for a woman is 36 – which means that a 36 handicap golfer, when playing a professional in a 'strokeplay' tournament, could score 36 shots more per round and still win, providing the professional returned a score for the complete round of at least one over par!

"The stroke index really comes into its own when playing matchplay, however. Let's assume you have a handicap of 18, and you are playing a match against a person with a handicap of 10. You should, therefore, receive 8 shots from your opponent. In matchplay, however, you win 'holes' rather than totalling your score for the complete round, and so it is deemed fairer if you are awarded three-quarters of the shots you should receive under your handicap. You would thus be given 6 shots, and you could use them on the most difficult holes on the course – that is, those with a stroke index of 1 to 6."

The par 3

I looked from the men's teeing ground down at the large green – the hole was par 3 and downhill – and looked inviting – until I noticed a huge bunker protecting the length of its front. "There has to be some obstacle in the way to prevent you from taking out your putter and putting your ball down the slope," said Nick. "Actually, this hole is more difficult than you might imagine. You've got to fly your tee shot all the way to the green. You shouldn't have too much trouble getting your ball to stop as you will be taking a lofted club and firing the ball in high. You will, however, have to be accurate."

I liked the look of the hole and waited impatiently for Nick to tee-off, except that he wasn't going to use a tee. "I'm only using an 8 iron here, and I prefer not to tee up my short or medium length iron shots. I'm aiming to achieve a lot of backspin, so I'll need to hit down and through the ball before taking a divot. That is why you'll find the teeing grounds on par 3 holes so very scarred." I waited while Nick took his shot which flew high in the air and dropped as light as a feather on to the green, spun back, and came to rest very close to the hole. I was impressed because, although Nick made it look so easy, I now knew how much skill was required to play such a shot.

"Did you notice how the wind got hold of that ball," said Nick. "This hole is in an exposed position and the wind, particularly on a blustery day like this, can play havoc with your tee shot. Luckily, I gauged the wind correctly and aimed my tee shot to the right. There is no real danger out there and, even if the wind had dropped suddenly, my ball should still have been in a good position, even if not on the green. The wind really can blow a golf ball about. It is one of the most unpredictable of the many variables you have to pit your wits and skill against when playing a round of golf. On the first hole, it wasn't so noticeable because the trees along the right-hand side of the fairway shielded us from it. Here the wind is blowing directly from right to left. Now,

Above: Studying the par 3 hole. Although the flag was merely 110 yards away, it had a huge bunker protecting the length of its front.

After a topped shot, I found myself in a bunker. Fortunately, the ball was not plugged in the sand and I was able to play a successful recovery shot.

the golden rule when playing in a wind is not to fight it but, if possible, let it work for you."

We arrived at the ladies' tee and I had to choose a club. The flag was about 110 yards away and Nick advised an 8 iron. "A nice, gentle, rhythmical swing should see you on the green from here," he said, "but rather than using a tee, let's see if you can play it straight from the turf. Find a nice clean area of the teeing ground, set yourself up, and swing smoothly. Remember to place the ball in the middle of your stance for an 8 iron shot, and to aim right to take account of the wind."

It wasn't the wind that was worrying me but the bunker which, from the ladies' tee, appeared to be even more massive. I set myself up with precision, aimed to the right of the target and swung, determined to get the ball high. The result was probably inevitable. I topped the ball and it scuttled with some velocity along the ground, down the slope, and into the belly of the waiting bunker. I moaned with frustration and admitted my error to Nick before he had time to point it out. "It's encouraging that you can analyse your own faults!" he observed. "If you know what you are doing wrong, then you are much more likely to rectify your mistake the next time the situation arises. Let's just hope the ball isn't plugged in the face."

Playing a plugged ball

We reached the offending bunker and, fortunately for me, found that the ball was not plugged but lying nicely on the flat having rolled up the face, and then back down. "If the ball *had* been plugged," said Nick, all you can do is try to dislodge it so that it rolls back down the bunker's face on to the flat. Then, at least, you will be able to play a real bunker shot even if, in the process, you have dropped one shot to earn the chance. Don't be too greedy. The worst possible thing you can do in such a situation is to *believe* that you can get the ball into the hole from such a lie. All that usually happens is that the ball stays where it is – or even more buried – and you find yourself swinging madly, totting up shot after shot in a frantic and increasingly desperate effort to get the ball out!

"If, however, the ball is plugged and you can get at it, then you've really got to hit down into the sand behind your ball with the face of your sand wedge open. This should enable the club to get deep enough to dig your ball out. You must, however, remember to *complete your stroke*. If you quit on your shot, then the ball will quit on you – and remain in the sand. But enough of this digression. Your ball certainly isn't plugged, and the shot facing you is simple. Let's see you get it to the very edge of the hole."

Getting out of another bunker

I followed the sequence he had taught me the week before. First, I tested the weight of the sand by shuffling my feet into it, then gave myself a firm, secure base from which to launch my swing. The sand was surprisingly light, considering the earlier shower, and I didn't think I'd have to swing very hard to shift the ball. "There's no reason why you shouldn't manage to get your ball pretty close," said Nick. "Even though you've had the misfortune to go into the bunker, you should be thinking 'par' from that position. One good bunker shot followed by a good putt and you'll have real cause for celebration: your first par score on an 18-hole course. You know you can play a good shot from there. Have confidence and concentrate. The only time confidence is out of place on a golf course is when it is based on foolish bravado rather than knowledge and technique – like when you try to hole a

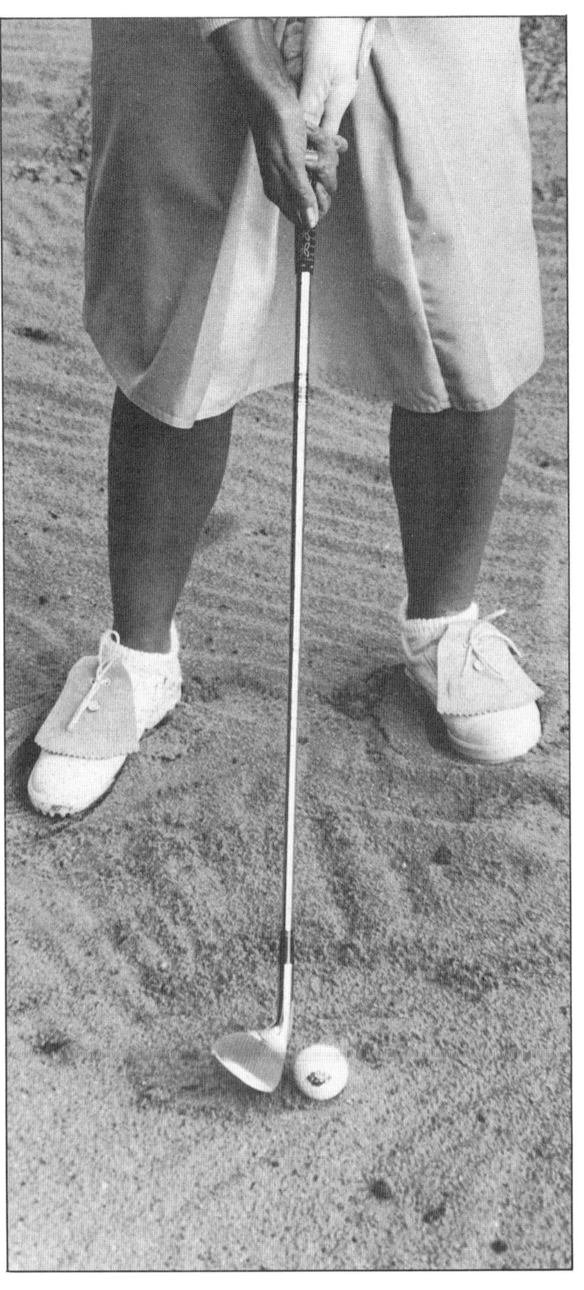

bunker shot when it is plugged deep under the lip!"

I focused my mind on getting the ball close. I picked a spot a couple of inches behind my ball and was careful not to let my sand iron touch the surface of the sand before swinging. "Open your stance a little," said Nick, "and remember to keep your legs nicely flexed." I concentrated on the point I had picked out behind the ball and swung. The wind blew the sand I had exploded out into my face and I couldn't immediately see the outcome of my shot – but I heard Nick's applause. There *was*, indeed, real cause for celebration. The ball had come to rest less than 2 feet from the hole. This time, however, I remembered to rake the bunker before gloating over my shot! This completed, I walked up on to the green and really felt elated. It was fantastic. All I now had to do was hole a tiny putt and I would have achieved par.

Nick's ball had made a pitch mark when landing on the green and, pointing out that it had to be repaired, he showed me how to do it. "You must always repair your pitch marks as a courtesy to the players following you around the course. Although they may repair your pitch marks if one is in the line of their putt to the hole, it's far more courteous if you repair your own. This is how you do it: take a repair prong or a tee peg – which you should always carry with you – and thrust it in at an angle under the indentation. Then lever up the squashed surface until it is level or slightly higher than the surface of the green. Finally, using the head of your putter,

Left: Test the weight of the sand by shuffling the feet in it, get a firm secure base from which to launch the swing and rake the sand after completing the shot.

gently pat down the area until it is firm and level."

My putt still had to be holed, and Nick pointed out that there might well be a nasty 'borrow' between my hole and the ball. I should also mark my ball, he said, because it could be in line with the putt he was about to attempt. "You've got a good opportunity here to see if there is any borrow, as my putt will travel along the same line as your much shorter one on its way to the hole." Handing me a small marker, he showed me how to mark my ball on the green – without leaving the marker directly in the line of his putt. He used his putter head to measure a distance from my ball, and then asked me to place the marker where he indicated.

He returned to his ball and lined up his putt, reminding me to watch the path of his ball. Nick's putt looked as if it was going to miss the hole by a good 12 inches, before it started curling in, teetering on the edge of the hole before gently dropping in. Now it was my turn and concentrating intently, I lightly stroked the ball into the hole.

There were, alas, only three par 3 holes, like the one I had just played on the course and Nick explained that golf courses are made up predominantly of par 4 holes. "This is because a par 4 presents the most challenge to a golfer," he said. "On a par 4, you have to play very well indeed to achieve a par, and superbly to get a birdie. A par 3 or par 5 doesn't present quite the same difficulty. It's true that to achieve a birdie on a par 3 you have to play two good shots, or one average shot followed by an excellent putt or vice-versa; but on a par 4 you have to, first, hit a good drive, then a good iron, and then a good putt. The par 5 is, perhaps, the easiest type of hole on which to achieve a birdie, because – if the weather conditions are favourable – it is possible to reach the green in two shots – which leaves you the luxury of two putts on the green. I think it's generally true to say that the par 4 hole offers the greatest challenge – and that is why there are more par 4s on golf courses than par 3s and par 5s.

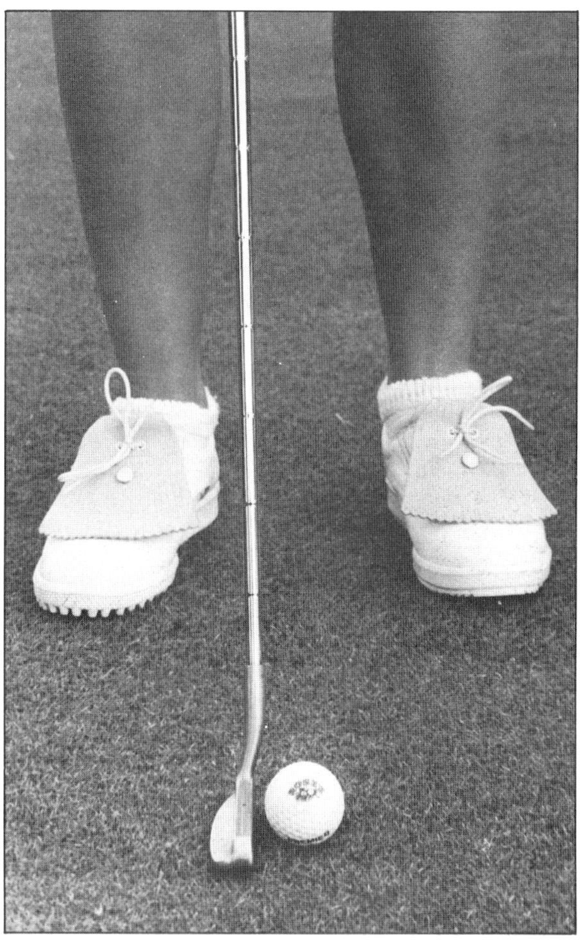

Above: Even on short putts it is important to relax and take your time. Check the line of the putt and gently stroke the ball into the hole.

Left: Using the 3 wood off the tee on the long par 5 hole *(right)*. Having teed the ball up as instructed, I aimed to sweep the ball away with the help of the 3 wood face.

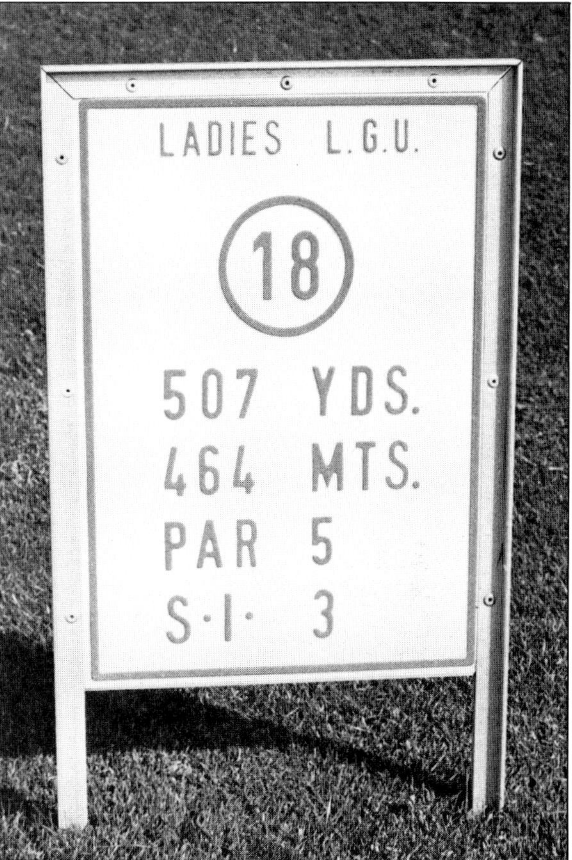

The par 5 hole

The par 5, however, was the next challenge I had to face. To the accomplished golfer, the par 5 is the easiest of holes, but to me, as a beginner, it looked disconcertingly long. I could barely see the green in the distance. "You'll soon gain confidence with long par 5 holes," reassured Nick. "This one is relatively simple as there is no 'dog-leg' to negotiate. You just have to play three good straight shots and you'll be on the green – providing you can miss the hazards on the way. There are one or two bunkers positioned to trap your ball on this hole, but, you'll be pleased to learn, no water hazards! I'll just tee off and then we'll talk about how I want you to play this hole."

I noted that Nick had taken his driver. He set himself up as usual – running through the routine he had taught me to use as a matter of course before each and every shot – and then really blasted one straight down the middle. Unusually for Nick, however, the ball began to slice away slightly and finished up a long way down the fairway, but just in the light rough along its right border. "I tried to hit that drive much too hard," said Nick, "and, as a result, swung slightly from 'out to in' and imparted slice on to the ball. Fortunately, it seems that I've just about got away with it – although it is much more difficult to control the ball when playing from light rough. I'll have to wait and see whether the ball is sitting up or lying down."

As we walked to the ladies' tee Nick explained how I should play the hole. "I see from the card," he said, "that this hole is 501 yards from the ladies' tee. Now, unlike me, don't try and be too greedy. Instead of using a driver, let's concentrate on getting you swinging confidently with your 3 wood. I'd like you to hit a smooth 3 wood right down the middle, and then, perhaps, we'll think about getting you to employ your 5 wood. We'll then get you hitting a middle iron into the heart of the green, and you'll then have two putts for par."

"The wind is blowing right behind you," said Nick, "so concentrate on *sweeping* that ball away. Don't try and make the ball rise, the angle on the face of your 3 wood will do that for you." I wanted to tee the ball up higher to achieve a shot with a higher trajectory. Surely this type of shot would have more chance of being blown further by the wind, I asked Nick. He disagreed. "Tee the ball up just as I instructed you, with half the ball showing above the face of your wood when you address the ball. If you tee the ball up high, you might well achieve your high trajectory, but it's more than likely that your ball will go high, but not far – even in this wind."

I teed the ball to regulation height and picked

out a target area on the fairway that seemed to stretch forever before me. I carefully went through the set-up routine, then tried to sweep the ball as smoothly as possible. The effect was dramatic. The ball soared into the sky and seemed to literally fly before the wind. It was an impressive strike, acknowledged Nick. "See what you can do with a good grip, a good set-up and a smooth swing," said Nick as we walked rapidly down the fairway, blown along by the strengthening wind. I merely nodded in reply, so intent was I on pacing out the drive I'd just hit. I

Pacing out the tee shot. In this instance, it was an impressive 227 yards, the longest drive I was to hit for some time to come.

knew it was the longest I'd ever struck, but also realised that it would probably be the longest I would hit for some time to come! I was determined to record it! We finally came to a stop at 227 yards.

"You'll be a danger to Laura Davies if you continue this sort of progress!" said Nick with a broad smile. "A ball has got to be struck very cleanly to travel that kind of distance. There's another golden rule in golf: When you've got good reason, blow your own trumpet. Believe me, there will be many days when you'll have nothing but a penny whistle to blow! Golf may be many things, but it's certainly not boring!" Just at that moment I was finding it absolutely exhilarating, and said as much.

Coping with an uneven lie

"Now, let's concentrate on your next shot. After that wonderful strike, I think you can risk a wood," said Nick. "Your only problem is that your lie is a bit uneven. When you address the ball, your feet are below the ball and it probably feels uncomfortable. All you have to do is stand further from the ball than normal as your swing will be flatter than usual. Don't try and change your swing, or pull yourself away from the ball. The adjustment we have made to your stance will compensate and you'll hit the ball cleanly." I observed that the shot might be easier with an iron. Nick disagreed, "Just swing your club smoothly and sweep the ball away."

I did as instructed but found the high ball very disconcerting. As I swung, I subconsciously pulled away – with the result that I not only topped the ball, but sliced it into the bargain. The ball skipped, hopped, bumped and made an ungainly swerve 40 yards or so into the light rough.

"Uneven lies take a bit of getting used to," said Nick. "When the ball is below your feet, you stand closer to the ball because your swing will be more upright. You have to make sure that you don't reach for the ball, otherwise you will find yourself hooking it. Uneven lies come in four unwelcome varieties! There is the 'ball above your feet variety' that you've just encountered. Normally, this type of lie causes the ball to fly to the left – the way the ground slopes. Somehow, you managed to defy the laws of gravity and got your ball to slice away against the grain to the right. Then there is the 'ball below your feet variety' which normally causes the ball to curve to the right; the downhill lie which causes the ball to fly low; and the uphill lie which causes the ball to fly high."

Up and downhill lies

Nick went on, "If the ball is on an uphill slope, then you should have the ball more forward in your stance at your address than normal – that is, nearer to your front foot. For the downhill lie, you should play the ball from further back in your stance – nearer your right foot. Only uphill and downhill lies should affect your club selection. If you are playing a downhill lie, then choose a more lofted club to help the ball into the air. Remember to let the club do the helping! I don't want to see you trying to lift the ball. On an uphill lie 'club up' – that is select a less lofted club. In other words, you should take a 6 iron instead of a 7 iron, for example, to prevent the ball from flying too high if on an uphill lie – unless you're playing with a howling gale behind you, and elevation is exactly what you want!"

In and out of the semi-rough

We reached our respective balls – which were keeping each other company in the fluffy semi-rough alongside the fairway. Nick said that my ball was sitting up rather too proudly. I questioned why that could possibly be a bad thing. "It's all too easy to scythe right under a ball when it's lying on fluffy stuff like this," said Nick. "The rule is, again, don't try to hit it too hard, even though it is sitting there apparently just asking to be whacked. You'll probably be best advised to take your 5 wood as well."

Nick's ball was not lying too badly and he managed to sweep it out of the semi-rough with what seemed a ridiculously easy swing. The ball flew high, was taken by the wind, and disappeared from sight between two fairway bunkers. "That's how you should swing a golf club – 'nice and easy'," said Nick. "You don't have to try and belt the cover off the ball for it to fly some distance – particularly when you've got a following wind – or in any conditions. I made an elementary and foolish mistake back there on the tee. When the wind is blowing directly behind you, there is always the temptation to try and lash a long one – particularly when you are trying to impress your playing partner! Resist that temptation. I was very lucky. If my ball had sliced a little more, I would have dropped at least one and possibly two strokes trying to get out of that stuff. You can learn through other people's mistakes as well as your own."

"Now let's see if you can sweep your ball out of this fluffy stuff with your 5 wood," he continued. "A good tip when your ball is 'sitting up' like that is to try and address the ball without grounding your club. This not only prevents the possibility of your ball toppling from its inviting lie into the depths of the semi-rough, but also helps to ensure that you don't swing *under* the ball. Pick out a point where you are going to hit your shot – between those two bunkers would be ideal – and swing smoothly." I addressed the ball without grounding my club, swung smoothly, and managed to sweep the ball cleanly off the grass but, alas, my old habit seemed to have returned. Although my ball started on line, it then sliced off line and ran into the fairway bunker on the right.

"Your grip is getting a little too weak," observed Nick, closely examining my fingers and knuckles. "That's why you are slicing. It may be tiresome, but you must check your grip before each and every shot. The grip really is all important – as you've just discovered. Check those two knuckles. You might think that it shouldn't be necessary but, believe me, it is. Even though I've played thousands of golf shots, I still check my grip. It's all too easy for that left hand to start creeping round the grip. But let's look on the bright side. You made very good contact with the ball, you've hit it quite some distance, and you're not in bad shape, as that bunker is very shallow and you shouldn't have any difficulty playing a middle iron from it. In addition, we've discovered why you sliced it in the first place. It's always gratifying to diagnose and rectify a fault early in a round!"

As we walked towards my ball I marvelled that such a tiny adjustment to the way you grip a golf club could have such a dramatic effect on what happens to the ball. I also thought how valuable it was having Nick with me to be able to tell me why a shot had not behaved as I intended. I wondered how beginners, who try and do without the advice of a professional, ever manage to get round a golf course with any golf balls still left in their bag, and their sanity intact!

Out of a fairway bunker

We reached my ball. "It's lying nicely on the surface," said Nick. "You've got about 100 yards still to go to the green, and I think you might get there with a 6 iron. Now, remember

Coping with an uneven lie where the ball is above the feet. The trick is to stand further from the ball than normal but without altering the swing in any way.

that you can't ground your club – and that is one of the things that makes playing from a fairway bunker a bit tricky. It is difficult to hold your club half an inch or so above the sand and maintain a smooth take-away on your backswing. Fortunately, however, there's hardly any lip to this bunker. You should set yourself up in exactly the way as if you were playing a 6 iron from the fairway – except that you are not allowed to ground your club. You'll need a full hip and shoulder turn for this shot, so don't open your stance. Also, try to clip the ball cleanly off the sand rather than hitting down and through the ball – so imagine you have a 5 wood in your hand and sweep the ball away."

I got in the bunker, shuffled my feet well into the sand, addressed the ball without touching the surface of the sand, and tried to clip the ball cleanly off the sand's surface. I succeeded. The ball flew towards the waiting green – which, unfortunately, was raised on a little plateau. My ball didn't quite have enough legs to climb this and came to rest at the bottom of a gentle slope. "Great shot!" said Nick. "If I had told you to use your 5 iron, then you might have got up that little slope. Mind you, it's quite possible that your ball

When the ball is 'sitting up' in the semi-rough *(right)* use a 5 wood and try to address the ball without grounding the club. In this instance, a weak grip caused me to slice the ball.

would have climbed the slope only to run off the back of the green. Sometimes, you can't win in this game!"

To pitch or chip?

We then walked up to Nick's ball which had very eloquently split the two fairway bunkers like an arrow, and was lying in the middle of the fairway about 50 yards from the flag. Nick looked carefully at the shot before him before saying, "As the green is raised I'll have to play a pitch from here. I can't afford to risk a chip and run, as there is no way of telling exactly how my ball will behave when it reaches that slope. So I'm going to 'fly' the ball right to the flag, and hope both that the green is receptive, and that I can impart enough backspin on the ball. I also want the ball to land softly, so I'm going to open my stance and aim to hit down and through the ball with the face of my pitching wedge slightly open." Nick played, translating theory into practice. His ball flew high, landed softly near to the flag, 'bit', and came to a rapid halt – leaving him no more than a 6 foot putt for a birdie. He appeared satisfied.

As we walked to my ball Nick advised me to play a small chip shot rather than a gentle pitch, saying: "You've got no real obstacles to negotiate, and the bank isn't steep enough to demand a really lofted club. Use your 7 iron, pick your landing circle, and run the ball up to the hole. If the flag was positioned much nearer to the edge of the green, I would advise you to use a pitching wedge because you would then be aiming to pitch on to the putting surface and stop the ball much more rapidly. The much higher trajectory of the shot you would play would help you to achieve the necessary soft landing. As you have a lot of green to work with, however, a chip is the right shot for this situation."

Once again I took the 7 iron from the bag, made sure that my grip was correct, formed an imaginary circle into which I wanted to chip the ball, and swung. Rather than a nice 'chunk' as my club made contact with the ball, I heard a nasty click, and looked up to see my ball scuttling up the bank along the ground and on to the putting surface. It ran a good 15 yards past the hole before finally coming to a stop. "You lifted your body at the top of your backswing," commented Nick, "and that caused you to hit the face of your ball with the front-leading edge of your club. The result could have been much worse. Luckily for you, the grass on the bank took some of the steam off the ball before it reached the green. If it hadn't, I think you would have been playing another chip shot from the other side of the green! Now see if you can putt the ball."

I was uncertain whether the putt was going to break to left or right but Nick was short on advice and suggested I work it out for myself. "I won't help you with the line of the putt, but remember what I said before – try and think of the hole as a 3-foot wide bucket." I looked closely at the putt before me and finally came to the conclusion that it would break from left to right. I picked the point where I thought the putt would start to turn, aligned myself square to that point, stroked the ball – and prayed! The ball didn't end up in the hole, but it did come to rest within Nick's '3-foot bucket', and I was able to hole my next putt with ease. I had scored a 7. If only I hadn't had an uneven lie with my second shot, I thought, but Nick reading my mind urged me on to the fourth tee, remarking that there were more 'if only's' in golf than in any other game.

We finally staggered off the 18th green about two and a half hours later. "Round in under 100 and no lost balls!" exclaimed Nick. "That really is a very impressive start. We'll soon have you consistently shooting in the low 80s. If you hadn't had that disaster in the bunker at the 15th, and gone out of bounds at the 17th – by which time you *were* beginning to flag a little – you would have shot under 90. Come on, let's go and have a drink, and then I'll see whether I can find a half set of clubs suitable for such a professional!"

I nodded my head and followed Nick towards the sanctuary of the clubhouse, tired but happy, and thinking: If only I hadn't driven out of bounds at the 17th – then I'd be *really* happy! It was, I suppose, an admission that I really was committed to the game of golf. Now, nothing would stop me attempting to improve my game and meet the challenges of the most exhilarating pastime I'd ever taken up.

Equipment

In the well-stocked pro shop, we talked about golf equipment.

"Unless you really want to impress your friends and have money to burn, it's not necessary to buy a complete set of clubs just yet," said Nick. "I would advise you to buy a half set such as this one." He showed me a half set consisting of a 3 wood, a 5 wood, a 3 iron, a 5 iron, a 7 iron, a 9 iron, a pitching wedge and a putter saying, "For the immediate future, this set should be perfectly adequate. Despite extravagant advertising claims, you don't need more expensive clubs than these, or a complete set until you are absolutely sure that you are going to continue with the game." I protested that I *was* sure.

"In that case," said Nick, "I'll put it another way. I think you will benefit by using fewer clubs. This is because you will have to improvise more and *feel* what a golf club is capable of achieving. Subtlety is an important part of the game of golf, and if you can make a club work for you, then you will rapidly become a very accomplished golfer. Play a few rounds with this setbefore thinking about moving up to a full set. Apart from anything else, you'll find them much lighter to carry around. It is also important to choose a matched set. You should feel in tune with your clubs, and it is much easier to achieve such harmony if all your iron clubs, especially,

Below: Aladdin's Cave of Golf shop displays the extensive range of golf clothing and equipment that is widely available today.

come from the same family. The set I am suggesting can be added to, if and when you decide that you've had enough of improvising with your 5 iron by gripping down the shaft to play a '6 iron' shot. Alternatively, you can trade them in – second-hand clubs are always in demand – and buy a complete matched set."

Checking the lie of a club

I looked at the clubs and they seemed very attractive after the clubs I'd been using. I said I'd buy them – but Nick cautioned me. "Don't be so hasty!" he said. "Let's make absolutely sure that these clubs are right for you before any money changes hands. The first thing I want to check is the lie of the club." I'd heard my former husband saying that he thought that the 'lie' of one of his clubs was a little suspect, but had never before had the technical interest to find out exactly what it meant.

Nick explained. He asked me to take up my normal address position and handed me a rather curious golf club. It had a moveable head which incorporated a gauge and a pointer. Making sure that my address position was abolutely correct, he checked to see whether the front-leading edge of the club was flat on the ground. He secured a screw to the head and looked at the gauge before telling me that he would have to adjust the clubs

Below: When choosing clubs, make sure they suit you personally. Your club professional will advise on the lie of the clubs to make sure they suit your stance.

slightly to make them perfectly suited to my stance. But how did he know that my clubs would need adjusting, I asked.

"The angle between the shaft of the club and the head must be exactly suited to your stance. If, when you address the ball, there is daylight between the heel of the club and the ground, then the toe of the club will stick into the ground at impact and cause you to slice. If, however, there is daylight between the toe of the club and the ground, then the heel of your club will stick in at impact and this will cause you to hook. The clubs I am suggesting you buy have a head that is slightly too flat for you, so they will need adjusting."

Nick told me the clubs were specifically made for women, their length being suitable for those of average height, like myself. He then asked me to test their weight and feel – which were fine – and the thickness of the grips. "Quite often, particularly with women, I find them using a discarded set of their husband's clubs with grips on them like elephant's tusks," said Nick. "It's no wonder they have difficulty playing the game. Thickness of grip really does make a difference. If the grip of your club is too thick, your wrist action will be restricted and there's a danger that you will push your shots out to the right; too thin, and your grip will become sloppy, and your control will suffer." The final equipment test was on the 3 wood, which Nick suggested I take outside and swing a few times to check the feel of it. Quite satisfied that it felt perfect, I had now only to choose a bag.

This was no problem. I'd had my eye on the

Left: Checking the weight and feel of a club, important factors in determining its suitability to an individual player.

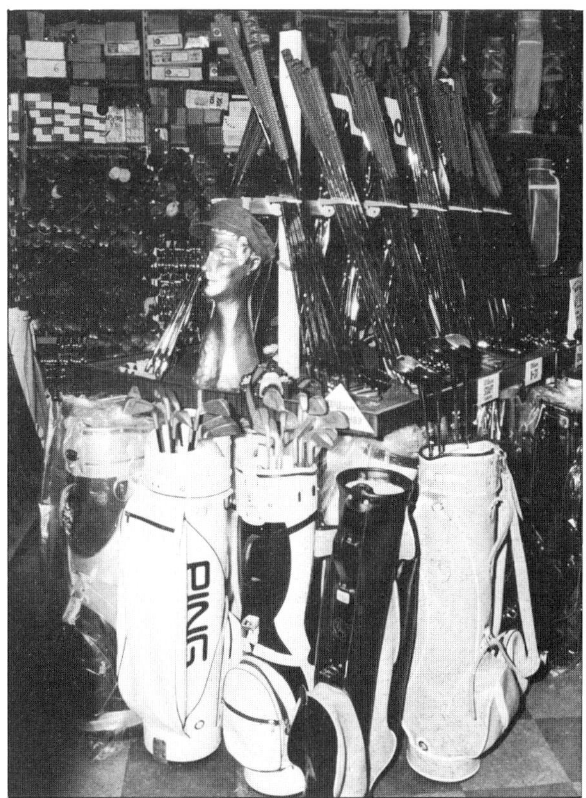

The well-equipped golfer also includes weatherproof garments in his or her kit, as well as clubs, balls, tees, markers and a pitch-repair fork.

very attractive yellow coordinated bag for some time. Nick agreed with my choice saying, "That's not only a very pretty bag, but also a very sensible one. It's lightweight, yet spacious and that is important. As well as your clubs, balls, tees, ball marker and pitch-repair fork, it's important to remember that there are certain other essentials you should carry in your bag before going out on the course. A golfing umbrella is a must, as is a waterproof suit which is loose enough to enable you to swing, but not too much so to impede your swing. It's also a good idea to carry a spare jumper with you at all times, and a pair of gloves or mitts during the colder months, as there is nothing worse than cold hands when trying to play golf! A cold head – as opposed to a cool head – can also be a great disadvantage, so I always carry a warm hat in my bag!"

Choosing golf balls

"A few years ago, I would have advised beginners to use the small ball," said Nick. "It flies much better in most conditions. Nowadays, most people prefer to play with the large ball, especially as most are sold with a no-cut guarantee." Thus advised, I chose the large, hard-covered ball and selected a bag of essential accessories before paying my money and leaving Nick's shop, the proud possesser of my first ever set of golf clubs.

Basic lessons over – on with the game!

That is how I learned the rudiments of golf, and gained an insight into how exciting it could be. The contents of this book can be used as a guide, but, once again, I'd like to stress that the book's main purpose is, not to provide you with a comprehensive instruction manual, but rather to encourage you, the reader, to *try* the game of golf. It is my firm belief that you will find it an enjoyable, invigorating, challenging and healthy pursuit.

If you do venture out on a golf course without first having lessons, you should, perhaps, know a little bit more about the etiquette of the game of golf, and some of the more basic rules. The two following sections are thus designed to provide you with no more than a short guide – so that you know the few essential do's and don'ts that should be observed.

Etiquette on the course

Etiquette on the golf course really means respecting your fellow players, and acknowledging that a golf course has to be maintained by you as well as talented groundstaff and greenkeepers if players are to get maximum enjoyment from its unique facilities.

Golf is also unique in that it is a game of trust. When out on the golf course, you will almost certainly be presented with countless opportunities to overlook the rules. Your ball, for example, may be lying in a particularly nasty bit of rough stuff. It is tempting to give it a small nudge on to some kinder terrain. If you do, only you – and the ethics of the game – will suffer. Remember, golf is a sport to be enjoyed, not a personal war against a small white, orange or yellow object that must be won at all costs. Play fair – and you'll enjoy the game.

On occasions, you will have an overwhelming urge to distract or unsettle a particularly irritating opponent. However, resist the temptation to rustle a crisp packet just as he/she is about to drive. Win by fair means, not foul, or don't play at all!

Wait for the players in front of you to move out of range before you play your shot. A golf ball is a hard little projectile. It can do great damage to people as well as greenhouse windows.

Replace all your divots.

Repair pitch marks on the green.

If you lose your ball, as happens frequently, remember you are only allowed five minutes to find it. If it is your last ball and you are not playing a match, wave other players through.

Hold the flag stick for other players when they are putting – if that is what they want.

Don't rush any of your strokes, but do try and move round the golf course as quickly as you can.

Always rake bunkers smooth after you have played a bunker shot.

Don't walk on the line of an opponents putt on the green.

Look after the course.

Display courtesy to your partner or opponent at all times.

A few vital rules

A complete guide to the rules of golf as drawn up by the R & A, St Andrews, can be obtained from your local pro shop. The few vital rules below relate simply to strokeplay.

On the teeing ground: You must place your ball either on a tee or directly on to the ground up to two club lengths behind the line of the tee you are on. The tee is the only part of the course where it is possible to make good the ground if you wish.

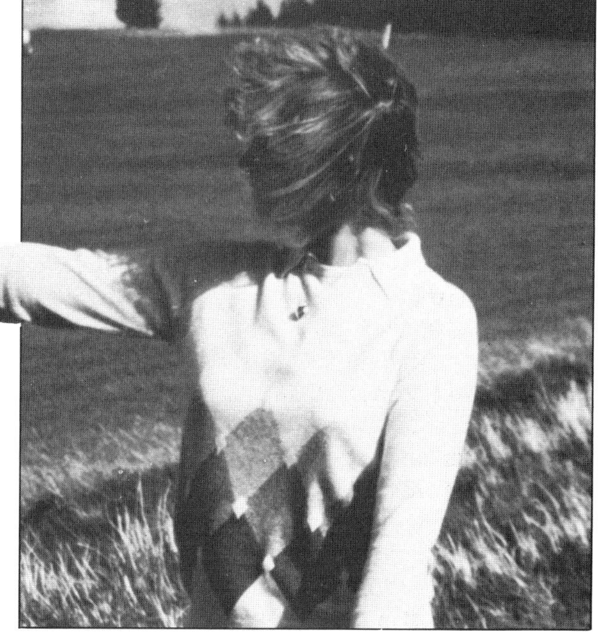

Above: Study the rules of golf to avoid unnecessary penalties. When dropping the ball, for example, stand straight and hold your ball at shoulder height.

Improving your lie: You may remove loose impediments such as stones, twigs etc., so long as you do not cause your ball to move. You are not allowed to meddle with anything growing to make your access to the ball easier, but you may move grass etc. to identify your ball.

Lost ball or out of bounds: If you think your ball may be lost or have gone out of bounds, you may play a provisional ball from your original position and take a 1-stroke penalty. If your original ball is found or has not gone out of bounds, the provisional ball you played is ignored. If you do lose your ball, you are not allowed to look for it for more than 5 minutes.

Unplayable ball: You can declare your ball to be unplayable anywhere on the course. If you do decide your ball just can't be played, you can take a 1-stroke penalty and drop the ball either within two club lengths of its original resting place, or anywhere along the original line of its flight – providing it is further back! If there is no suitable place to drop your ball (in thick woods, for example), you must replay your original shot for a penalty of two shots.

Dropping the ball: When you 'take a drop', you must stand straight and hold your ball at shoulder height. When you drop the ball, it must not touch you or your equipment on the way down. You should try and drop the ball as near to its resting place as possible, but not nearer to the hole. If your ball rolls into a hazard, out of bounds, or rolls more than two club lengths from where it landed, you may re-drop without penalty. If the ball rolls into such a position twice, you may then place it where it first struck the ground when re-dropped.

Placing your ball: If your ball refuses to stay where placed, you may replace it without penalty. If your ball continues to roll, you may then place it where it will stay at rest, but, again, not nearer to the hole.

Playing the wrong ball: This is easier to do than it may sound, and carries severe penalties! If you play the wrong ball, even by accident, you lose two strokes. It is wise to mark your ball distinctively before playing.

Cleaning your ball: You can only clean your ball when on the putting green, when you lift under penalty, or when you are fortunate enough to lift without penalty (when the ground is under repair, for example).

Changing your ball: You can only change your ball once you have started to play a hole if it is so damaged that its flight would be affected. The new ball may be placed where the original ball was without penalty.

Taking a free drop: You may take a free drop if your ball lies on or so close to an immovable object that it is impossible for you to play your shot. You may take a free drop one club length away from the object, though not nearer the hole. Some examples of where you may take a free drop are casual water, ground under repair, and if your ball comes to rest in a hole made by a burrowing animal.

When you are in a hazard: The most important rule to remember is that you must not ground your club when addressing the ball. This not only includes bunkers, but also water hazards (if the water is shallow enough for you to have a realistic chance of hitting the ball)! You are not allowed to lift your ball for identification in a hazard.

What about the flagstick?: You can decide whether to have the flagstick left, attended, or removed. If, however, you do accidentally hit the flagstick with your ball when it is attended or removed, you then incur a 2-stroke penalty. The same occurs if you hit a person or piece of equipment.

On the green: You may repair pitch marks and remove loose impediments on the putting green such as leaves, twigs, sand, etc. You may remove your ball and clean it – provided you mark its position first. If your ball is on the putting line of another player's ball, you should move your ball one or two putterheads to the side whilst he or she putts. In strokeplay, if your ball hits that of an opponent, you lose two strokes – so ask your playing partners to mark their balls if you think they are on the line of your putt!

Scoring: In competition, you are responsible for recording the scores of the player whose card you have been given to mark. You should check his

Above: In competition golf, you mark your opponent's card, recording the score after each hole. On completing the round always check and sign your own card.

or her score after each hole before you record it. After the round has finished, you sign the card and hand it to the player. You are also responsible for checking your own score card when you receive it from your marker, who should also have signed the card. When the card is checked by the committee (in a tournament) a score recorded lower than actually taken results in disqualification; a score higher than taken must stand as returned.

Who plays first?: The player who has just won the last hole normally tees off first. Thereafter, the player who is farthest from the hole plays first.

Taking practice swings: You may take practice swings at any time – except when you are in a hazard.

What size ball?: The R & A governs weights, size and velocities. It is still possible in the UK to choose between the small (1.62 in) and the large (1.68 in) ball. There is, however, a move towards using the larger ball which is legal everywhere.

How many clubs?: You may carry a maximum of 14 clubs in your bag, including the putter. You are not allowed to borrow clubs during the course of a round, but it is permissible to replace a club damaged during the normal course of play. If, however, you deliberately damage a club, you may not replace it. Bad temper isn't encouraged on the golf course. Remember golf is a game to be enjoyed!

Above: Remember you must not carry more than 14 clubs in your bag, including the putter. You can, however, replace a club damaged during normal play.

Glossary of golfing terminology

Address – The position a golfer takes up before swinging the club.
Airshot – A failed attempt to strike the ball.
Albatross – A score of three under par, this is most likely to occur on a par 5 hole.
Apron – The area of grass immediately surrounding the green, where the grass is kept slightly longer than on the green.
Arc – The path of the club through the swing.
As it lies – The ball should always be played 'as it lies' unless it is deemed by the rules to be unplayable, relief is allowed or the ball is lost.
Backswing – The initial movement away from the ball made with the club.
Baseball grip – One of the three conventional methods of gripping the club where the hands are close together but do not overlap or interlock.
Birdie – A score of one under par.
Blind – The word used when a golfer is forced to play a hole with the green out of sight, or a shot where natural obstructions restrict the player's view of his/her target line.
Bogey – A score of one stroke over par. A double bogey is two strokes over par, and so forth.
Bunker – A hazard consisting of a prepared hollow of ground filled with sand. *Note*: A golfer is not permitted to ground his/her club before playing the shot.
Bye – This refers to the number of holes left to play when the match is over. If, for example, one party wins the match three and two, the bye is the remaining two holes left to play.
Caddie – From the French *cadet*, meaning page, later referring to people in search of work such as carrying and conveying messages in Scottish cities; thus, the word came to mean 'porter'. Today, it refers to the person who carries the player's clubs during play.
Carry – The distance a ball travels in the air.
Casual water – Water that accumulates temporarily on the golf course as a result of heavy rain or flooding, also snow and ice. The rules of golf state that if a player's ball lands in casual water, he/she is permitted to drop the ball clear without penalty.
Chip – A short, low shot played to the green.
Cock – This refers to the action of bending the wrists at the top of the backswing.
Concede – In matchplay, a player may concede a hole when she considers herself to have lost it, or alternatively she may concede a putt when her opponent is so close to the hole that it would be impossible to miss.
Cup – The hole which houses the flagstick.
Dead – A shot or putt which leaves the ball so close to the hole that it would be impossible for the player to miss the putt.
Divot – A piece of turf removed from the ground by the player when taking a shot. All divots should be replaced so that the course remains in good order.
Dormie – In matchplay, a player is dormie if he/she is leading by as many holes as there are left to play e.g. if a player was five holes ahead with five to play, he/she would be dormie five.
Double eagle – The American equivalent of an albatross – that is, a score of three under par.
Draw – A shot played with spin so that the ball moves slightly right to left.
Drive – The shot played from the tee, usually with a driver.
Duff – A player 'duffs' a shot when he/she accidentally hits the ground behind the ball.
Eagle – A score of two strokes under par.
Face – The surface on the clubhead used for striking the ball.
Fade – A shot played with spin so that the ball moves slightly left to right.
Fairway – The area of cut grass between the tee and the green.

Feathery – One of the original golf balls stuffed with feathers and leather-bound.
Flagstick – Also known as the 'pin', it is a moveable pole with a flag that is placed in the hole to indicate its position.
Follow through – The path of the club after striking the ball.
Fore (or take cover) – A cry of warning to a fellow player who is in danger of being hit by the ball travelling towards him/her.
Fourball (or better ball) – In which two partners team up and the lower score at each hole counts.
Foursome – A way of playing golf when two partners team up and play alternate shots with the same ball.
Free drop – Under certain conditions, the rules of golf make provision for a free drop without penalty.
Green – The putting surface.
Grip – This refers to the position of the player's hands on the club, as well as to the grip itself which is the leather or rubber area at the top of the club or shaft.
Ground under repair – An area of ground deemed unplayable and from which a player may drop clear without penalty.
Halved – In matchplay, a hole or match is halved when each player has taken an equal number of shots to complete the hole or round.
Handicap – A system of allowing all players of varying abilities to compete on equal terms. If the standard scratch score of a particular golf course is 72, a scratch player should complete his/her round in 72. A 10 handicap golfer should return a score of 82 and a 24 handicap golfer in 96 strokes. He/she then subtracts the handicap from the gross score resulting in the net score.
Hazard – Any bunker, pond, stream or ditch.
Hole – The hole is 4½ inches (108 mm) in diameter and at least 4 inches (100 mm) deep.

Above: When putting you can choose to have the flag, or pin as it is also called, attended or removed. The hole itself is 4½ inches (108mm) in diameter.

Holing-out – Striking the ball directly into the hole.
Honour – The player or side entitled to drive first from the tee is said to have the honour. The honour goes to the player or side who has had the lowest score at the preceding hole.
Hook – A shot which bends sharply to the left.
Hosel – The point where the shaft connects with the clubhead.

Glossary of golfing terminology

Interlocking grip – Where the little finger of the right hand links the first finger of the left.
Ladies' tee – The tee designated for the use of women golfers, usually closer to the hole than men's tees.
Lateral water hazard – Water, whether a ditch or stream, running parallel to the hole, signalled by red stakes or lines.
Lie – The area on which the ball finally stops.
Line – The intended direction of the ball to the hole.
Links – Once referred to the strip of land or 'link' between the mainland and the sea. Today, it describes seaside golf courses.
Lip – The edge of the hole.
Local rules – Rules relating to a specific course, in addition to the Rules of Golf as set out by the Royal and Ancient Golf Club in St Andrews, Scotland.
Loft – Refers to the angle of the clubhead and dictates the varying heights and distances a ball can fly.
Loose impediments – These are natural objects such as twigs, leaves, stones, worms, casts etc. that can be moved.
Lost ball – A ball is deemed lost if it has not been found after five minutes of searching.
Matchplay – The fewest strokes played wins the hole in matchplay and the winner is the player who finishes more holes ahead than there are left to play.
Medal play (also called strokeplay) – The player records his/her score at each hole and totals them on completion of the round.
Municipal course – A course open to the public and owned and run by the local authority. Known as a public course in the U.S.A.
Net – A player's score after he/she has deducted the handicap from the gross score.
Out of bounds – Ground on which play is not permitted, indicated by stakes or a fence. If a player hits a ball out of bounds he/she incurs a two stroke penalty. However, a ball is only out of bounds when all of it lies out of bounds and it is permissible for a player to play a shot from a position out of bounds while the ball is lying in bounds.
Par – The score allocated to a hole or the sum total of holes. Par is determined by a hole's yardage.

For women
A hole of up to 200 yards is par three.
A hole of up to 400 yards is par four.
A hole of over 400 yards is par five.

For men
A hole of up to 250 yards is par three.
A hole of up to 475 yards is par four.
A hole of over 476 yards is par five.

Penalty – Applies to a ball that is either lost, unplayable or out of bounds and incurs a penalty for the player. Penalties can also be applied to any players infringing the rules in other ways.
Pitch – A short, high shot played to the green.
Play-off – When two or more players tie a match, this will lead to extra holes being played in order to decide an outright winner.
Plugged ball – A ball which buries itself in its own pitch mark.
Preferred lie – Rules devised for wet or wintery conditions which allow the player to lift, clean and place the ball in a better position without incurring a penalty.
Provisional ball – A ball played when the original ball is thought lost, out of bounds or outside a water hazard. If the player continues to play with that ball, it is no longer deemed provisional. However, if the player finds the original ball the provisional ball is abandoned.
Pull – A shot that moves without spin to the left of the target.

Push – A shot that flies without spin to the right of the target.
Putting green – The ground laid out specifically for putting.
Rough – The area of the course that has not been cut away or mown.
Round – This refers to the complete 18 holes of the course.
Rub of the green – Any outside influence on the ball bringing the player either good or bad luck.
Sand iron (or sand wedge) – An extremely lofted club designed to strike the ball out of a bunker.
Scorecard – The card that a player should fill in during stroke play. It is also completed by the player's partner or opponent and signed by both players.
Scratch – Refers to the player who continually plays to the par or standard scratch score of a course, therefore affording him/her a handicap of scratch.
Shank – This occurs when a player mis-hits the ball by striking it too close to the hosel and thus causing it to fly off sharply to the right.
Short game – Pitch and chip shots.
Slice – A fault arising in the swing causing the ball to fly left to right.
Sole – The surface of the club that rests on the ground upon address.
Stance – By placing the feet in the correct position, the player is 'taking a stance' in preparation for making a stroke.
Stroke index – A chart on the scorecard which indicates the holes where a handicap player is entitled to handicap strokes.
Sudden death – The extra holes that two or more players must play in order to produce an outright winner.
Swing weight – The weight of a clubhead when a player swings a club.
Tee – A peg normally made out of plastic or wood on which the ball is placed in order to drive off. Also refers to the area known as 'the tee' or teeing ground.
Top – Caused by a player striking the top of the ball so that it fails to fly through the air; instead, it runs along the ground.
Vardon grip – So called because it was associated with Harry Vardon. The little finger of the right hand overlaps the first finger of the left.
Water hazard – Refers to the sea, lake, river, pond or ditch or surface drainage and is defined by yellow stakes or lines.

Useful addresses

English Golf Union
1/3 Upper King Street
Leicester
LE1 6XS

Tel: (0533) 553042

English Ladies' Golf Association
PO Box 14
52 Boroughgate
Otley
West Yorkshire
LS21 1QW

Tel: (0943) 464010

Golf Foundation
78 Third Avenue
Bush Hill Park
Enfield
Middlesex
EN1 1BX

Tel: 01-367 4404

Ladies' Golf Union
12 The Links
St Andrews
Fife
KY16 9JB

Tel: (0334) 75811

Ladies' Professional Golf Association
1250 Shoreline Drive
Suite 200
Sugarland
Texas 77478
USA

Tel: 713 980 5742

Royal and Ancient Golf Club
St Andrews
Fife
KY16 9JD

Tel: (0334) 72112

Women's Professional Golf Association
Apollo House
The Belfry
Sutton Coldfield
West Midlands
B76 9PT

Tel: (0675) 70333

Bibliography

Books

AA, The, *AA 1986 Guide to Golf Courses in Britain*, AA Publications, 1985

Alliss, Peter, *Play Golf with Peter Alliss*, Collins, 1985

Alliss, Peter, *The Golfer's Logbook*, Collins, 1984

Alliss, Peter, *The Shell Book of Golf*, David and Charles, 1981

Alliss, Peter, *The Who's Who of Golf*, Orbis, 1983

Armour, Tommy, *How to Play Your Best Golf all the Time*, Hodder and Stoughton, 1954

Barton, Pamela, *A Stroke a Hole*, Blackies, 1937

Blake, Mindy, *The Golf Swing of the Future*, Souvenir Press, 1972

Chamberlain, Peter, *Good Golf*, Queen Anne Press, 1985

Charles, Bob, *The Bob Charles Left-hander's Golf Book*, Angus and Robertson, 1985

Cossey, Rosalynde, *Golfing Ladies*, Orbis, 1984

Cotton, Henry, *Thanks for the Game*, Sidgwick and Jackson, 1980

Cotton, Henry, *This Game of Golf*, Country Life, 1948

Dobereiner, Peter, *Golf Rules Explained*, David and Charles, 1985

Galway, W. Timothy, *The Inner Game of Golf*, Jonathan Cape, 1981

Hawtree, F.W., *The Golf Course*, E. & F.N. Spon Ltd, 1985

Hay, Alex, *The Handbook of Golf*, Pelham Books, 1985

Henderson, Ian T. and Stirk, David, *Compleat Golfer*, Victor Gollancz, 1985

Hogan, Ben, *The Modern Fundamentals of Golf*, Kaye and Ward Ltd, 1957

Houghton, George, *Golf Addicts to the Fore!*, Gordon Wright Publishing, 1985

Irwin, Hale, *Play Better Golf*, Octopus, 1980

Jacobs, John, *Golf Doctor*, Stanley Paul, 1979

Jacobs, John, *Play Better Golf*, Stanley Paul, 1969

Jacobs, John, *Practical Golf*, Stanley Paul, 1972

Maclaren, Muir, *The Golfer's Bedside Book*, Reed Book Pty Ltd, 1976

Mair, Levine, *The Dunlop Lady Golfers' Companion*, Eastland Press, 1980

McDonnell, Michael, *The Complete Book of Golf*, The Kingswood Press, 1985

Nicklaus, Jack, *My 55 Ways to Lower Your Golf Score*, Hodder and Stoughton, 1965

Player, Gary, *Gary Player's Golf Secrets*, Pelham Books, 1964

Professional Golfers' Association, *Know the Game*, A & C Black Publishers Ltd, 1985

Ryde, Peter, *Golf*, A & C Black Publishers Ltd, 1976

Saunders, Vivien, *The Complete Woman Golfer*, Stanley Paul, 1975

Saunders, Vivien, *The Golfing Mind*, Stanley Paul, 1984

Stirling, John, *The Skills of the Game*, The Crowood Press, 1985

Taylor, J.H., *Taylor on Golf*, Hutchinson, 1902

Trevino, Lee, *I Can Help Your Game*, Star, 1982

Wilson, Enid, *Golf for Women*, Barker, 1964

Magazines

Golf Illustrated

Golf Monthly

Golf World

Index

All numerals in *italics* refer to illustrations.

Index

Acknowledgements

Photographs and illustrations
I would like to thank the following for supplying material for use in the book:

Aladdin's Cave of Golf Shop: pages 126, 127 and 129
BBC Hulton Picture Library: pages 9, 11, 14, 17, 31 and 32
Peter Dazeley Photography: pages 10, 19, 20, 21, 22, 23, 24, 25, 26, 27, 28 and 29
Mary Evans Picture Library: pages 13 and 30
Alan Roberts: front and back covers, and pages 34 and 96
Phil Sheldon: page 33 (left and right)

The illustrations and diagrams on pages 39 (top right), 42, 58-9, 94 and 101 are by Terry Evans.

The illustrations on Pages 7 and 8 are taken from Heath Robinson's *Humours of Golf* and are reproduced by courtesy of Gerald Duckworth & Co Ltd.

All other photographs are by Phil Silcock.

My thanks to 'Sports Pages' of New Compton Street, London, for their help in compiling the bibliography.

Aladdin's Cave of Golf
If you would like further information on the clothing and equipment featured throughout the book, or would like to visit Europe's largest golf shop, please contact the staff at:

Aladdin's Cave of Golf
31-34 Windsor Street
Uxbridge
Middlesex

Tel: (0895) 33080 or 51691